MATTHEW ARNOLD

MEN AND BOOKS

MATTHEW ARNOLD

by

J. D. JUMP

LONGMANS, GREEN AND CO

LONDON . NEW YORK . TORONTO

MGE

LONGMANS, GREEN AND CO LTD
6 & 7 CLIFFORD STREET LONDON W I

BOSTON HOUSE STRAND STREET CAPE TOWN
531 LITTLE COLLINS STREET MELBOURNE

LONGMANS, GREEN AND CO INC
55 FIFTH AVENUE NEW YORK 3

LONGMANS, GREEN AND CO
20 CRANFIELD ROAD TORONTO 16

ORIENT LONGMANS LTD
CALCUTTA BOMBAY MADRAS
DELHI VIJAYAWADA DACCA

First published 1955

PRINTED IN GREAT BRITAIN
BY WESTERN PRINTING SERVICES LTD., BRISTOL

TO

BARBARA

PREFACE

IN this book, I have tried to interpret and to reassess the achievement of Matthew Arnold. My view of what is of greatest importance in it differs from that of most of my predecessors in that I am unable to regret his switching from poetry to criticism in early middle life. This view is in harmony with opinions expressed from time to time by Mr. T. S. Eliot, Dr. F. R. Leavis, and Mr. F. W. Bateson. But none of these has made Arnold the subject of a full-length study; and most of the principal Arnoldians—Professor Lionel Trilling, Professor Louis Bonnerot, Sir E. K. Chambers, Professor E. K. Brown, Professor C. B. Tinker, and Dr. H. F. Lowry, for instance—seem to rate his poetry very much more highly than I. In praise of his criticism, on the other hand, it is likely that I go at least as far as they could wish.

I am happy to acknowledge my indebtedness to the various critics and scholars who have preceded me in this field, and especially to those named in this preface and in my bibliography. I owe much, for example, to Professor Trilling in my discussion of Arnold's youthful dandyism; to Dr. Lowry in my consideration of his friendship with Clough; to Dr. Leavis in my assessment of his poetry; and to Professor Bonnerot and Professor E. D. H. Johnson in my analysis of 'Empedocles on Etna'. But a conscientious examination of other critics' opinions, backed by an elaborate apparatus of notes, would have been quite out of place in a work intended mainly for the non-specialist. I trust that this general expression of indebtedness will make amends by its prominence for what it lacks in detail.

I wish to acknowledge also the considerable help I have received from friends and colleagues. In particular, I am deeply grateful to Professor G. L. Brook, Professor L. C. Knights, Dr. R. G. Cox, and Mr. Christopher Hanson for agreeing to read the work in typescript and for allowing me to profit by their criticism and advice. I wish also to thank Miss Leila Hourani for typing the greater part of the text.

For permission to reproduce copyright material, I make acknowledgement to the following: Messrs. Faber and Faber Ltd. and Random House Inc. for an extract from 'Look, Stranger' from *Collected Shorter Poems* by W. H. Auden (originally published in America in the volume *On This Island*, copyright 1937 by W. H. Auden); Oxford University Press for extracts from *The Poetry of Matthew Arnold* by C. B. Tinker and H. F. Lowry, and *The Letters of Matthew Arnold to Arthur Hugh Clough* edited by H. F. Lowry; and Miss Dorothy Ward and Messrs. William Collins Sons and Co. Ltd. for material from *A Writer's Recollections* by Mrs. Humphry Ward.

CONTENTS

ILLUSTRATIONS

THE MAN

I

THE trustees who, in December 1827, elected Thomas Arnold, at the age of thirty-two, to the headmastership of Rugby had been assured by one of his supporters that he would, if appointed, change the face of education all through the public schools of England. This he was indeed to do. At that time, Eton, under Keate, was an atrocious despotism, devoted to pedantry and often close to anarchy; but Rugby, under Arnold, was rapidly to become the earliest of the modern public schools and to serve as an example for the rest. Arnold achieved this result partly by administrative and curricular reforms. He gave a good share of responsibility for the government of the school to the sixth-form boys; he improved the status of the assistant masters; and he added modern history, modern languages, and mathematics—all, admittedly, in small quantities—to the regular classical course of study. But his triumph was due above all to his personal qualities, to his energy and determination. He succeeded in teaching the school subjects to the senior boys in such a way as at one and the same time to turn out good classical scholars, to awaken their historical imaginations, and to instruct them in politics and Christian ethics. Both in these lessons and in his impressive sermons in the school chapel—in fact, in all his dealings with Rugby—he had a clearly conceived end in view: to make the school a centre of what he believed to be genuinely Christian training. Never, in fact, would he tolerate any suggestion that education might be divorced from religion.

Possessed by a profound sense of the sinfulness of human nature, especially in childhood, Arnold was a strict disciplinarian. He demanded from his pupils a high standard of conduct and of moral thoughtfulness, and he let slip no opportunity of impressing upon them, and upon the members of his sixth form in particular, the gravity of their responsibilities. His younger pupils found him a stern, aloof, and awe-inspiring figure. But the older boys, having learned to make allowance for his shyness and his quick temper, came to know him better and to regard him with affection, pride, and reverence.

A few of them, however, allowed their responsibilities as members of his community to weigh much too heavily upon them. Thus, Arthur Hugh Clough, one of his favourite pupils, could write at the age of seventeen, 'I verily believe my whole being is soaked through with the wishing and hoping and striving to do the school good.' Youth ought surely to be encouraged to carry itself more lightly than this. Arnold, inculcating moral earnestness, quite forgot, as one of his admirers pointed out, that it was God Almighty's intention that there should exist between childhood and manhood the natural production known as a boy. On most of Arnold's pupils the effect of this oversight must have been slight enough— and not altogether harmful, either. But on an intelligent, scrupulous, and anxious youth such as Clough the effect could be lasting and disabling. It is not fanciful to relate to it the fatigued joylessness of Clough's maturity.

Clough himself seems to have suspected something of the kind. His *Dipsychus* is a poem dramatizing the dilemma of one torn between the promptings of a tender conscience and those of a worldly wisdom. The 'Epilogue' to it consists of a prose dialogue between the poet and his uncle, who holds that his nephew's generation is too scrupulous and too pious. 'It's all Arnold's doing; he spoilt the public schools. . . . Not that I mean that the old schools were perfect, any more than we old boys that were there. But whatever else they were or did, they certainly were in harmony with the world, and they certainly did not disqualify the country's youth for after-life and the country's service.' He brushes aside his nephew's protest and goes on to describe the Rugby product as 'a sort of hobbadi-hoy cherub, too big to be innocent, and too simple for anything else. They're full of the notion of the world being so wicked and of their taking a higher line, as they call it. I only fear they'll never take any line at all.' When the nephew tries to excuse Arnold, the uncle exclaims, 'Why, my dear boy, how often have I not heard from you, how he used to attack offences, not as offences—the right view—against discipline, but as sin, heinous guilt, I don't know what beside! Why didn't he flog them and hold his tongue? Flog them he did, but why preach?' In reply, the nephew invokes the spirit of the age. 'If he did err in this way, sir, which I hardly think, I ascribe it to the spirit of the time. The real cause of the evil you complain of, which to a certain extent I admit, was, I take it, the religious movement of the last century, beginning with Wesleyanism, and culminating at last in Puseyism. This over-excitation of the religious sense, resulting in this irrational, almost animal irritability of consciences, was, in many ways, as foreign to Arnold as it is proper to——' The uncle is bored, however, and the conversation ends. Obviously, the uncle's views were not Clough's. But they were held by many men at that time; and Clough evidently felt that there might be some truth in them.

Arnold's move to Rugby in August 1828 detached
him from the village where he had lived since shortly
before his marriage to Mary Penrose eight years earlier.
This village was Laleham, on the Thames between Staines
and Chertsey, about eighteen miles above London. Here
he had at first conducted a small private school in part-
nership with his brother-in-law; subsequently, he had
concentrated upon coaching a few senior boys—not more
than about nine at a time—for the university. Just before
leaving for Rugby, he had expressed the fear that he would
there miss the 'absolute play', the gymnastics and bathing,
which he had enjoyed with these youths. Still worse was
the fact that the midland countryside was less varied and
attractive than that of the Thames valley, which he loved.
After he was installed at Rugby, he explained his distaste
for the view eastwards from there by asserting that in
that direction there was nothing fine between the observer and the Ural mountains!

His passion for natural scenery was, indeed, Arnold's
strongest aesthetic emotion. Despite his warm admiration for Wordsworth, both as a man and as a writer, his
taste in poetry was narrow. Nor did he write it with
any skill; years later, his son Matthew remarked sadly
on seeing a specimen of his verse: 'Ah, my poor father!
he had many excellencies, but he was not a poet.' He
himself admitted his insensibility to painting and music.
His passion for natural scenery, however, was one of the
great forces in his life. In alliance with his devotion to
history, it led him to spend his holidays travelling not
only in England but also in France, Italy, Spain, Switzerland, and Germany—his elder children accompanying
him on some of his later Continental tours; and in 1832
it led him to acquire Fox How, a small estate near
Ambleside, within easy reach of the Wordsworths.

(Indeed, the poet himself helped him to obtain it.) Here, among the mountains and streams he loved, he and his family began to spend the school holidays. Before long, the grey stone house there had become their true home.

A letter which he wrote during Matthew's last year at school gives a glimpse of them engaged in winter sports during one of these holidays. 'Wordsworth is remarkably well, and we see him daily; and moreover, Rydal Lake is frozen as hard as a rock, and my nine children, and I with them, were all over it to-day, to our great delight. Four of my boys skait. Walter is trundled in his wheelbarrow, and my daughters and I slide, for I am afraid that I am too old to learn to skait now. My wife walks to Ambleside to get the letters, and then goes round to meet us as we come from the Lake.'

Arnold was an enthusiastic walker. He and his wife would set out almost daily from their Rugby home, she riding on a small, quiet pony, preferably a grey one, while he strode along beside her at over four miles an hour, talking freely on history and politics as he did so. When, in the Lake District, a larger party set out, his activities were more various: he comforted any children who might tumble, encouraged those who lagged behind, and was throughout a cheerful and judicious guide. He took a keen pleasure in wild flowers; towards the end of his life he was to speak of 'the deep delight with which I look at wood anemones or wood sorrel'.

Arnold loved to join in his children's games. During the summer holiday of 1835, which had to be spent partly at Rugby itself, he greatly enjoyed cricketing with Matthew and his brothers 'on the very cricket ground of the "eleven," that is, of the best players in the school, on which, when the school is assembled, no profane person may encroach'. Those who had known him only

at Rugby, and who were unaware of such vacation
escapades as this, were often surprised on first witnessing
his tenderness and playfulness in the home circle. Presumably they expected the great headmaster, with his
intense moral fervour, to be a solemn domestic tyrant.
And, though their error was grotesque, there is no doubt
that Arnold was a formidable parent. The moral
strenuousness and the severity which enabled him successfully to evolve, from the English public school, a more
intelligent and more conscientious, if occasionally more
priggish, product must have been evident likewise in his
home. But equally evident must have been the vigorous
enjoyment of living, the boyish good spirits, and the
prompt sympathy recorded by those who knew him more
intimately.

He was not merely a headmaster and a parent, however. He was also an eager and lively participant in the
political and religious controversies of his time. 'I must
write a pamphlet in the holidays,' he told his sister during
one crisis in public affairs, 'or I shall burst.' His outlook
was Liberal. Politically, he supported Catholic Emancipation and Parliamentary Reform and sympathized with
the moderate French Revolution of 1830. In religious
matters, his Liberalism was so marked that the more
dogmatic young J. H. Newman could ask with some
asperity, 'But is *he* a Christian?' and Wordsworth, con-
fiding to Henry Crabb Robinson that he loved Arnold,
could add that he was 'a *good* man, & an admirable
schoolmaster, but . . . would make a desperate bad
bishop'. His Liberalism exposed him more than once
to violent Tory abuse; and it would not be surprising to
learn that in consequence his senior pupils' attachment
to him grew even stronger.

Arnold was indebted to Samuel Taylor Coleridge more

than to anyone else for his views on Church and State.
'I think', he said, 'with all his faults old Sam was more of
a great man than any one who has lived within the four
seas in my memory. It is refreshing to see such a union
of the highest philosophy and poetry, with so full a
knowledge, on so many points at least, of particular
facts.' Following Burke, Coleridge had insisted that the
state, in addition to its negative function of protecting
the individual from undue interference by his fellows,
the positive duty of humanizing and civilizing its
bers. His defence of the established church rested
his conviction that in its ideal form an endowed
isy' was the organ by which the state fulfilled its
ational and spiritual responsibilities.

rnold amplified these doctrines and, since he was
ve all a practical man, strove actively to realize, both
his own tiny province of Rugby and in England as a
le, that ideal of a highly disciplined Christian com-
nity to which they seemed to him to point. He per-
ded the trustees, in 1831, to allow him to be school
plain as well as headmaster; in the outside world,
ilarly, he insisted upon the absolute identity of the
church and the state. For was not the highest welfare
of man the aim of both? The state could not accomplish
this without the wisdom and goodness of the church, nor
the church without the sovereign power of the state.
The two societies were, or ought to be, one. Utilitarians
and others who favoured a merely secular state earned
his loathing; so, too, did the Tractarians, with their
priestly claim that the church was wholly independent
of the secular power. Against such as these, Arnold
laboured for the abolition of all distinction between
spiritual and secular, for the complete identification of
Christian with political society.

B

But the actual established church was the church of only a portion of the population; outside it, there was a vast body of dissenters. If it was to become a truly national church, a truly effective society for putting down moral evil, making its spiritual influence felt even in spheres hitherto held to be purely secular, it had to be made more comprehensive. This it could become if its doctrine were reduced to that which is acceptable to all Christians, if its constitution were made more dem cratic, and if the various services of the sects wei conducted, at different hours, in the same parish chur By these means, virtually the whole population cou brought into the one fold, and Christianity could bec the recognized basis of citizenship.

It is evident that the author of these proposals rega creeds and rituals as of less importance than good de In his eyes, Christianity was above all a system for seminating morality. Indeed, he defined religion 'nothing more nor less than a system directing influencing our conduct, principles, and feelings, professing to do this with sovereign authority, and m efficacious influence'. This being so, he was not frig ened by the German Biblical criticism of which, thanks partly to 'old Sam', he became aware rather earlier than most English scholars. For his faith was not based upon intellectual beliefs such as criticism might undermine.

Arnold's willing acknowledgment of the sovereign power of a state which should be also in its spiritual aspect the national church anticipates his son's elevation of the state above the social classes which he saw competing for supremacy. His wish to unite the Christian sects in a comprehensive established church and his conviction that religion is predominantly morality are likewise echoed and developed in Matthew Arnold's works. But, even when they are engaged in similar undertakings, the tone of the two men's writings is widely different. Father and son may share certain debating tricks—for example, the telling reiteration of an opponent's word or phrase—but whereas the son's tone is bantering and ironical the father's is earnest and urgent. This is well seen in the following passage (originally contributed to a Sheffield newspaper), in which Thomas Arnold follows Coleridge in stressing society's responsibility for humanizing and civilizing its members, and anticipates Matthew's persistent concern with th total human perfection of his fellows:

A man sets up a factory, and *wants hands*: I beseech y to observe the very expressions that are used, for th significant. What he wants of his fellow creat loan of *their hands*;—of their heads and hear nothing. These *hands* are attached to certai and bodies which must be fed and lodged: but th done as cheaply as possible;—and accordingly, up miserable row of houses, built where ground is cheap t, that is, where it is least generally desirable to get it;—built as close as possible, to have the more of them on a given space, and for the same reason without any sort of garden or outlet attached to them, because the comfort and enjoyment of the human being is quite independent of the serviceableness of his *hands*. But further, Sir, these *hands* are not only attached to mouths and bodies, but to reasonable minds and immortal souls. The mouths and bodies must be provided for, however miserably, because without them the hands cannot work; but the minds and souls go utterly unregarded. And is this any other than a national crime, a crime in the civil government, a crime in the church, a crime in all the wealthy and intelligent part of the English people, that while *hands* have been multiplying so enormously during the last forty years in every corner of the kingdom, no greater efforts have

been made to provide for the welfare of the human beings
who have multiplied with them; beings born not for time
only but for eternity [?] (*Letters on the Social Condition of the
Operative Classes*, X).

Matthew Arnold, then, inherited both the profound
respect for the idea of the state and the Broad Church
liberalism of his father. Very largely from the same
source, no doubt, he acquired his taste for travel and his
love of the countryside in general and of mountains and
streams in particular. But he was no mere docile heir.
The characteristic difference in tone of the two men's
writing is indicative of important differences in character
and personality. These should become evident later.

In 1841, Thomas Arnold was offered the Regius Professorship of Modern History at his old university,
Oxford. No public reward or honour could have been
so welcome to him, and he accepted it with joy. 'I
caught at any opportunity of being connected again with
Oxford;' he wrote to a friend whom he had known as
an undergraduate, 'and the visions of Bagley Wood and
Shotover rose upon me with an irresistible charm.'
Moreover, there were the Tractarians, with their glorification of priestcraft, to be combated. His intention was
to resign the headmastership of Rugby at the end of
1842 and to retire to Fox How, making his professorial
visits to Oxford from there. But these plans were never
to be carried out. In the summer of 1842, he died
suddenly from an attack of *angina pectoris*, a disease apparently inherited from his father and transmitted to his
son Matthew.

His widow, who outlived him by thirty-one years,
made Fox How her home for the remainder of her life.
Five years his senior, Mary Arnold was a charming,
sympathetic, and intelligent woman devoted to her

husband during his life and to his memory after his death. Yet this devotion did not result in her binding herself immovably to his opinions. 'She had a clearness and fairness of mind,' wrote Matthew in reply to a letter of condolence, 'an interest in things, and a power of appreciating what might not be in her own line, which were very remarkable, and which remained with her to the very end of her life.' Her reception of her son's *Literature and Dogma* (1873) seemed to him to testify to an openmindedness quite astonishing in a woman past eighty; it was also characteristic of one who remained to the end in close contact with contemporary thought. During her earlier years at Fox How she was a great favourite of the Wordsworths; after the poet's death, she was one of the only three persons who could tempt the aged Crabb Robinson as far afield as the Lake District. Matthew's weekly letters to her are those of a correspondent who knew that he could count upon her full comprehension over the whole range of his interests.

II

Mrs. Arnold's family was large; and, of the ten children born to Thomas Arnold and herself, five sons and four daughters reached adult life. Matthew, born on 24 December 1822, was their second child. He was a year younger than Jane, who was to become his favourite sister and the first reader, or hearer, of his poems. Jane, an intelligent girl, evidently inherited her father's spirit and determination. As a child of three, she refused on one occasion to curtsy to her mother, 'persisting in her disobedience for two hours in spite of the corner and other tokens of our displeasure, her little heart swelling with pride'. This behaviour made her father consider, rather ponderously, 'how truly pride is our original and besetting sin from the first'. The incident foreshadowed a severer conflict. Shortly before his death, Jane contracted what he thought an imprudent engagement with one of his assistant masters, and he felt obliged to forbid it. Despite this early attachment and its frustration, Jane had from 1850 onwards a very happy married life. Her husband was W. E. Forster, a manufacturer of Quaker upbringing who became a respected Liberal politician and is remembered for his important Education Act of 1870. In 1849, Matthew had acknowledged Jane's 'passionate hopes' and ardour in his poem 'Resignation', which he had dedicated to her as 'Fausta'. Throughout his life, she remained, as 'K', one of his favourite correspondents. 'You and Clough are, I believe,' he assured her in 1859, 'the two people I in my heart care most to please by what I write.' His letters to her contain many friendly messages to a well-liked brother-in-law.

Matthew spent much of his early childhood at Laleham. The large old red-brick house with the wide lawn flanked by cedars was his home until his father took up his appointment at Rugby. Two years after this move, Matthew returned to the district of his birth in order to begin his formal education under the uncle with whom his father had once worked. During all this time there was developing in him that love of the Thames valley which he never lost. Visiting Laleham in early manhood, he recorded with pleasure that he 'found the stream with the old volume, width, shine, rapid fulness, "kempshott,"[1] and swans, unchanged and unequalled, to my partial and remembering eyes at least'.

His father, too, had a hand in his early education, teaching Latin to Jane, Matthew, and Thomas, the third

[1] A facing of piles and boarding along the bank of a river.

child. But a fresh stage was reached when, at the age of thirteen, Matthew was sent to Winchester, his father's old school. He stayed there only one year. In August 1837, after a holiday with his parents in Paris and other places in northern France, he was transferred to Rugby, where he remained until 1841.

Glimpses of Matthew during his schooldays reveal a child who is recognizably the father of the man. At Winchester, he coolly informed the headmaster that he found the work quite light; not surprisingly, he paid dearly for the pleasure of this remark at the hands of his indignant fellows. At Rugby, where he was seen to be 'very reserved' and known as 'Lofty Mat', his mockery is said to have been directed on at least one occasion, and without its victim's knowledge, upon Dr. Arnold himself. For even as a boy Matthew did not permit himself to appear too much in earnest. His flippancy worried his parents. 'Matt likes general society,' said his father, 'and flitters about from flower to flower, but is not apt to fix.' With an austere literalness, his father tried to restrain his lively sallies. Even so, a neighbour had to record in a letter that, although to her the sons seemed delightful boys, Mrs. Arnold felt that they were not all that 'their Father's children ought to be' and that they did not exhibit 'the sobriety of mind and manliness of character she had a right to expect from their training. Matt's passion for fishing is as strong as Henry Fletcher's. He is not to be allowed to go to College unless he shows a more decided sense of duty in his school work the next half year.'

Matthew's passion for fishing lasted long. But in spite of it his school work must have improved; for in the autumn of 1841, after a holiday with his father and his brother Tom in the south of France and the Pyrenees, he

entered Balliol College, Oxford, as a classical scholar.
Here his activities were in part such as ought not to have
surprised those who knew his athletic father. They may,
however, have surprised those who remembered the
small boy whose parents had been worried by his ill-
health and by the clumsiness which had resulted from
his having had his legs in irons for nearly two years. He
went out with the harriers. He achieved a leap over the
Wadham railings which was long known to many who
remained ignorant of his books. He boated on the
Cherwell and elsewhere. Above all, he found time to
wander in the Cumnor hills with his particular friends
Clough and Theodore Walrond and his own brother Tom.

During the vacations, he walked, boated, and skated
in the Lake District. There he saw a good deal of
Wordsworth, knowing well how to draw out the old
poet in conversation. Those who found it strange that
the eldest son of the practical and prosaic headmaster
should win the poetry prize at Oxford, as previously at
Rugby, may have been tempted to ascribe his success to
the influence of the Poet Laureate. But Matthew was in
many ways an unexpected product of the Arnold home.

At Fox How, the young people produced a family
magazine. Comments in this make it clear that the
eldest son was something of a dandy, elegant and supercilious. Jane was responsible for a ballad about a 'fine
young Oxford gentleman' who 'wears an eye-glass round
his neck hung by a silken string':

Eau de Mille Fleurs, Eau de Cologne and twenty eaux
    beside
Rowland's Odonto, scented soaps, jostle his books aside.

At Oxford, Matthew was quite a social lion and worried his more scrupulous friends, and particularly the

old Rugbeians among them, by his jaunty demeanour, his
affectations, and his idleness. While allowing himself
filially to echo Dr. Arnold's liberalism in the headquarters
of Newman, he evidently wished to avoid seeming too
much his father's son, even to the extent of flaunting
tastes and attitudes directly opposed to those of his
parents. One of his contemporaries years later described
him as having been

> So full of power, yet blithe and debonair,
>   Rallying his friends with pleasant banter gay,
> Or half a-dream chaunting with jaunty air
>   Great words of Goethe, catch of Béranger.

His friends appreciated his cheerfulness, geniality, and
kindliness; but they had their fears. 'Our friend Matt',
wrote one of them while they were both still under-
graduates, 'utters as many absurdities as ever, with as
grave a face, and I am afraid wastes his time considerably,
which I deeply regret, but advice does not go for much
with him, and perhaps I am not well qualified to give it.'
Perhaps Matt resented it, too. At all events, when they
went together on a trip to Devonshire in 1843, the same
friend reported that they arrived only 'after sundry dis-
plays of the most consummate coolness on the part of
our friend Matt, who pleasantly induced a belief into the
passengers of the coach that I was a poor mad gentleman,
and that he was my keeper'.

At length it began to appear that the indolent Matthew
might not only fail to reach the first class but even drop
below the second class in his degree examination. In
July 1844, he retired to Patterdale in the Lake District
to read for it under Clough's supervision. But before
long Clough was reporting to a correspondent: 'For this
evening, Mat is away; a party of Oxford visitants from

Ambleside and Grasmere came over last night to spend
the weekly holiday; hospitalities were required, slow-
doms to be borne with: so Mat improvised a necessity
to visit his Penates, and left the *onus entertainendi* upon
me, departing after Morning Services. . . . I left Liverpool last Monday; slept at Fox How. Mrs. Arnold was
well and kind, but somewhat anxious about Mat. . . .
Mat has done something this week, but this foolish walk
today will lose him all tomorrow I have no doubt. . . .
I am painfully coerced to my work by the assurance that
should I relax in the least my yoke-fellow would at once
come to a dead stop.' Things were no better ten days
later: 'Matt has gone out fishing, when he ought properly
to be working, it being nearly four o'clock . . . it has,
however, come on to rain furiously; so Walrond, who is
working sedulously at Herodotus, and I, who am writing
to you, rejoice to think that he will get a good wetting.'
Three weeks before the examinations began in the
autumn of the same year, he became very diligent. 'I
think', wrote Clough, 'he is destined for second; this is
above his deserts certainly, but I do not think he can
drop below it, and one would not be surprised if he rose
above it in spite of all his ignorance.' A week later, he
repeated this forecast, adding, 'May he also tread in my
steps next Easter!'

This is precisely what Arnold did. Like Clough three
years earlier, he redeemed his second as an undergraduate
at Balliol by a fellowship at Oriel. During the months of
waiting, Wordsworth, whose own college career at St.
John's, Cambridge, had been undistinguished, is said to
have taken him under his special protection. Arnold
spent the time teaching the lower fifth form at Rugby
under Dr. Tait, his father's successor. Evidently his
mischievous sense of fun was not damped down either

by his recent rebuff or by his current labours. At a masters' meeting, Tait observed that strict Calvinism devoted thousands of mankind to be eternally———. He paused. Obligingly, Arnold supplied the word which the headmaster's delicacy had prevented him from uttering: 'Damned!' A burlesque examination of conscience follows his report of this incident to Clough.

Among his younger colleagues at Rugby was one whom the respectable and censorious accused of dressing with an unseemly gaiety and of riding to hounds in term time. Nevertheless, he had been made a housemaster. Calling on him one day, Arnold found him conducting with trepidation his first entertainment of parents, a breakfast with a staid couple who had entrusted their son to his care. No doubt, the parents were pleased to meet the eldest son of the late headmaster, a tall, graceful young man with a strong face but a languid manner and with whiskers and wavy hair as black as coal. He sat down at the table with them but fastidiously waved aside the dishes which their host offered to him. 'No thank you, my darling,' he said casually, 'I've just bitten off the tails of those three bull-pups of yours, and that does take the edge off one's appetite.' Revelling in the resultant consternation, he went on: 'By the way, I had a look at that mare of yours when I was in the stable. I'd advise you to have her vetted before you ride her to hounds again.'

In the summer of the year in which he was elected to the fellowship, Arnold visited the Isle of Man with his mother and his sister Jane. In the summer of the following year, 1846, he went further afield. At Oxford, during the regular Sunday morning breakfasts in Clough's rooms, Clough himself, Walrond, and the two Arnolds had, of course, discussed everything under the sun. But they had concerned themselves particularly with George

Sand, of whom Clough and more especially Arnold were passionate devotees. Her novels breathed a spirit of emancipation; and there was an enjoyable defiance of conventional susceptibilities involved in preferring them to the edifying works of Mrs. Trimmer or Hannah More. In 1846, Arnold determined to see the George Sand country and, if possible, to meet the authoress herself. By rail and stage-coach he made his way to Boussac in the centre of France. Recalling, thirty years later, his visit to her Château of Nohant, he wrote:

From Boussac I addressed to Madame Sand the sort of letter of which she must in her lifetime have had scores, a letter conveying to her, in bad French, the homage of a youthful and enthusiastic foreigner who had read her works with delight. She received the infliction good-naturedly, for on my return to La Châtre I found a message left at the inn by a servant from Nohant that Madame Sand would be glad to see me if I called. The midday breakfast at Nohant was not yet over when I reached the house, and I found a large party assembled. I entered with some trepidation, as well I might, considering how I had got there; but the simplicity of Madame Sand's manner put me at ease in a moment. She named some of those present; amongst them were her son and daughter, the Maurice and Solange so familiar to us from her books, and Chopin with his wonderful eyes. There was at that time nothing astonishing in Madame Sand's appearance. She was not in man's clothes, she wore a sort of costume not impossible, I should think (although on these matters I speak with hesitation), to members of the fair sex at this hour amongst ourselves, as an out-door dress for the country or for Scotland. She made me sit by her and poured out for me the insipid and depressing beverage, *boisson fade et mélancolique*, as Balzac called it, for which English people are thought abroad to be always thirsting,—tea. She conversed of the country through which I had been wandering, of the Berry peasants and their mode of life, of Switzerland whither I was going; she touched politely, by a few questions and remarks, upon England and things and persons English,—upon Oxford and Cambridge, Byron, Bulwer. As she spoke, her eyes, head, bearing, were all of them striking; but the main impression she made was an impression of what I have already mentioned,—of *simplicity*, frank, cordial simplicity. After breakfast she led the way into the garden, asked me a few kind questions about myself and my plans, gathered a flower or two and gave them to me, shook hands heartily at the gate, and I saw her no more. (*Mixed Essays*, 'George Sand'.)

On George Sand, Arnold made the effect of a young Milton on his travels, 'l'effet d'un Milton jeune et voyageant'. Did he perhaps tell her more about his 'plans' than was known to most of his English acquaintances, to whom his first volume of poems two and a half years later came as something of a surprise?

It has been plausibly conjectured that they must also have talked, in connection with Switzerland, of Étienne Pivert de Senancour, who had died during that year, and who was admired by both of them as the author of *Obermann*. This work, a series of letters written from the solitude of the Bernese Oberland and treating almost entirely of nature and of the human soul, was valued by Arnold for its profound inwardness, its austere sincerity, its delicate feeling for nature, and its melancholy eloquence. It expressed the *mal du siècle* and related it correctly to those forces in contemporary life which tended to promote it.

Arnold must have wished to see the various places associated with Obermann; and when he did visit them the countryside charmed him for life. But he did not go to Switzerland at once. Instead, he returned to England.

In London, he had his first sight of the great French tragic actress, Élisa Rachel, in the part of Hermione. He became immediately an enthusiastic admirer of her art and followed her to Paris. Arriving there on 29 December 1846, he saw her in Corneille's *Polyeucte* on the same evening and attended every one of the ten or more performances she gave during his stay of slightly over six weeks. He found time also for French lessons, for dancing, and for visits to other theatres. His love of play-going was to remain with him for life. But no other actress, not even Sarah Bernhardt, was ever to rival 'the divine Rachel' in his estimation.

Back at Oxford, he must have seemed as much of an exquisite, as mannered and as conceited, as ever. Clough reported: 'Matt is full of Parisianism; Theatres in general, and Rachel in special: he enters the room with a chanson of Béranger's on his lips—for the sake of French words almost conscious of tune: his carriage shows him in fancy parading the Rue de Rivoli; and his hair is guiltless of English scissors: he breakfasts at 12, and never dines in Hall, and in the week or 8 days rather (for 2 Sundays must be included) he has been to Chapel *once*.' In addition to these un-English habits, he had brought back some notable waistcoats. Another contemporary, who must first have seen him at about this time, remembered him as a handsome young man, 'strong and manly, yet full of dreams and schemes. His Olympian manners began even at Oxford; there was no harm in them. . . . The very sound of his voice and the wave of his arm were Jovelike.'

In the spring of the same year, 1847, he became private secretary to Lord Lansdowne, the influential Whig statesman. The appointment made Tom apprehensive, presumably because he felt that it might accentuate his brother's worldliness. Certainly, Matthew had now to live in the metropolis; and there he mixed freely with wealthy, talented, and sophisticated people. When his sister Mary visited him in London in 1849, and his mother in 1850, they seem to have feared that his social engagements would leave him little time to see them. If so, they were pleased to discover their mistake; and Mrs. Arnold found her son affectionate and 'unspoiled by his being so much sought after'. He was well liked by Lord Lansdowne.

Naturally he still gave himself airs. In his letters he refers to himself and his chief as 'me and my man'. He was still drawn to 'the life without'. A shopping-street was the best place in which to consider the question of the format of a projected volume of poems by two friends. He was still a dandy. Crabb Robinson enjoyed having him to breakfast, finding him 'a very gentlemanly young man, with a slight tinge of the fop that does no harm when blended with talents, good nature & high spirits'. Charlotte Brontë, however, took a sterner view. Meeting Arnold at Fox How, she found his appearance striking and prepossessing but was displeased by his 'seeming foppery' until she discerned beneath it a real modesty and 'some genuine intellectual aspirations'. On this occasion, Arnold talked at length with both Charlotte Brontë and Harriet Martineau 'and sent the lions roaring to their dens at half-past nine'. Clearly, the young man who had in the previous year spoken of the 'Flibberti-gibbet, fanatical, twinkling expression' of his godfather, John Keble, had still not learned to revere the famous.

III

If a chanson of Béranger's made an effective addition to an English dandy's ensemble, and if it was possible to shock the unco' guid by praising George Sand, it must not be supposed that such considerations exhausted the value of these writers for the young Arnold. Béranger expressed an epicureanism which in certain moods he found highly congenial. George Sand voiced a cry of agony and revolt, a trust in nature and beauty, and an aspiration towards a purged and renewed human society with which, too, he could sympathize. Senancour was, for his romantic melancholy, still closer to him than either of these.

Nor was his interest in modern literature confined to that written in French. He acknowledged Wordsworth's healing power, his ability to bring men back into contact with natural things. While his admiration for Byron had slightly diminished since he had written his Rugby and Oxford prize poems, he was still deeply stirred by the passionate and titanic defiance of eternal law uttered by the poet whom Goethe had represented as Euphorion in the second part of *Faust*. Goethe himself he already recognized as the greatest of the modern in his wise, profound, and comprehensive criticism of life.

Forty years later, recalling the voices which had most charmed him during his Oxford days, he spoke of the salutary novelty of the large, liberal view of human life in Goethe's *Wilhelm Meister* to the Englishman of that time; but he went on to say that what had then moved him most deeply had been its poetry, its eloquence. Carlyle's, too, had been an eloquent voice, until he had so sorely strained and abused it. Early in 1848, discussing a recent article by Carlyle, Arnold could couple an admission of the commonplace nature of the thoughts with warm praise for 'the style and feeling by which the beloved man appears'. Eighteen months later, however, Carlyle seemed to him a moral desperado; and ten years later still his eloquence was 'that regular Carlylean strain which we all know by heart and which the clear-headed among us have so utter a contempt for'. The third of the influential voices had been that of Emerson, and Arnold always retained his high regard for a sage whose service to the human spirit he could compare with that of Marcus Aurelius. The last voice had been that of one of the four people from whom Arnold, reviewing in middle life the whole of his development and not merely his Oxford years, was conscious of 'having learnt—a very different thing from merely receiving a strong impression—learnt habits, methods, ruling ideas, which are constantly with me; and the four are—Goethe, Wordsworth, Sainte-Beuve, and yourself'. John Henry Newman, the recipient of this tribute, had been a leader of the party in Oxford which Arnold's father had detested for its glorification of priestcraft. Nevertheless, he so charmed his opponent's son that towards the end of his life Arnold could write:

> Forty years ago he was in the very prime of life; he was close at hand to us at Oxford; he was preaching in St. Mary's pulpit every Sunday; he seemed about to transform and to renew what was for us the most national and natural institution in the world, the Church of England. Who could resist the charm of that spiritual apparition, gliding in the dim afternoon light through the aisles of St. Mary's, rising into the pulpit, and then, in the most entrancing of voices, breaking the silence with words and thoughts which were a religious music,—subtle, sweet, mournful? . . . Or, if we followed him back to his seclusion at Littlemore, that dreary village by the London road, and to the house of retreat and the church which he built there, . . . who could resist him there either, welcoming back to the severe joys of church-fellowship, and of daily worship and prayer, the firstlings of a generation which had well-nigh forgotten them?
> (*Discourses in America*, 'Emerson'.)

C

Arnold was not the only old Rugbeian to feel Newman's charm. But in him the influence showed itself not in the acceptance of a more completely Catholic doctrine but in the development of certain habits of mind. A contemporary reviewer perceived something of this when he said years later that Newman and Arnold were alike as prose-writers in their luminous, urbane, delicately expressed dogmatism and in their irony which tended to run into caricature.

The young man who was receiving and pondering these influences, who at Oxford attended the meetings of the Decade, a debating society which counted among its members Benjamin Jowett, Arthur Stanley, and Clough, and who in 1850 could report that amid much other reading he had been studying Spinoza and finding his atmosphere positive and vivifying, was clearly more than the fop he chose to seem. The same may be said of the correspondent who urged upon Clough one of the greatest of the Hindu scriptures, the *Bhagavad Gita* or 'Lord's Song'. In part, Arnold's dandyism was the product of youthful exuberance; some of the stories told to illustrate it refer to mere practical jokes. Moreover, it served to demonstrate his independence of his father. A third motive, perhaps more important than either of these, is traceable in the letters which he wrote to his friends, and above all to Clough, during this period.

Clough, nearly four years his senior, had entered Rugby in 1829. He had been a gentle, sensitive, affectionate, and highly intelligent boy of rather delicate health. His parents were living in America; and Dr. Arnold had soon become not only a schoolmaster but also in many ways a father to him. On his side, the homeless Clough had grown somewhat too deeply attached to his school and its headmaster, with the result that his natural scrupulousness had been greatly over-stimulated. Academically, he had made excellent progress, and in 1837 he had gone up to Oxford accompanied by the very highest hopes and expectations of all who knew him. These he was to disappoint, though not in any spectacular fashion.

At this time Oxford was profoundly disturbed by the Tractarian movement. In the resultant atmosphere of restless religious speculation, Clough became puzzled, bewildered, and unsettled. His failure to secure a first in his degree examination in 1841 was a natural, though unexpected, consequence, which he redeemed a few months later when he was elected to an Oriel fellowship. By this time Arnold had come up from Rugby, and Clough's schoolboy acquaintance with him quickly ripened into a warm adult friendship. At the Sunday morning breakfasts in his rooms and at the meetings of the Decade, Clough could be voluble, buoyant, brilliant. 'I can talk tremendous!' he once admitted. His friends acknowledged his charm. At the same time, he was still the anxious, scrupulous soul whom the Tractarian controversies had so shaken; and in 1848 he resigned his fellowship because he could not sincerely subscribe to the Thirty-nine Articles of the Church of England. After a continental tour which led him to Paris during the Revolution of 1848 and to Rome during its siege by the French in 1849, he returned to England to take up the post of Principal of University Hall, London—a nonsectarian residence for students which Arnold characteristically nicknamed 'Doubting Castle'. In 1852 he resigned this post. There followed a nine-month search for suitable employment in America, after which he settled down to an examinership in the Education Office in London. In 1859 his health began to fail. Further

extensive travels could not restore it, and in 1861 an
attack of malaria at Florence hastened his death.

During Arnold's years at Oxford and at Lansdowne
House, Clough was his closest friend. Thereafter, for
the last ten years of Clough's life, they remained on good
terms, though without the old intimacy. As young men,
they shared many interests. They were ambitious to
prove themselves poets, and they were enthusiastic
classicists. They delighted to explore together the
countryside around Oxford. They were keenly interested
in social and political problems.

Clough, indeed, was something of a radical. At all
events, Arnold could address a letter in 1848 to 'Citizen
Clough, Oriel Lyceum, Oxford' and by so doing give
him a nickname which stuck to him for months. Despite
this teasing, Arnold went some distance in political
sympathy with his friend, though not, he insisted, so far
as to delude himself with unrealizable hopes. The mil-
lennium, he assured Clough, wouldn't come this bout.
At Lansdowne House, his interest in public affairs was
being greatly stimulated. He had every opportunity there
of keeping himself well informed and was accustomed to
report and to discuss the latest news in his letters. Those
to Clough during the early part of 1848 contain a running commentary on events in France. In this connection
Arnold was led to speak for the first but by no means for
the last time of the '*wide and deepspread intelligence*' which
'makes the French seem to themselves in the van of
Europe'. When the poet Lamartine achieved a brief
political eminence, his remarks were in a lighter vein.
'My man [*i.e.*, Lord Lansdowne] remarks that Poets
should hold up their heads now a Poet is at the head of
France. More clergyman than Poet, tho: and a good deal
of cambric handkerchief about that. No Parson Adams.'

Domestic affairs interested him, too. He went to hear the speakers at the Chartist convention in the spring of 1848 and was much struck by their ability. He had no doubt that he was living in a time of social revolution and that, as he told his mother, 'hereditary peerage and eldest sonship and immense properties' could not last much longer. At the same time, the state of the English masses was such that he could not without some apprehension regard the prospect of their asserting themselves. On the Irish problem, his views were already close to those which he advanced at length later in life.

But, if Clough and he agreed politically 'like two lambs in a world of wolves', Arnold could not accept the view of poetry which Clough's work seemed to him to embody. Admittedly, Clough's sincerity was unmistakable. It was evident that he was striving to get breast to breast with reality. But in Arnold's opinion this effort cost him too much. There was a 'deficiency of the *beautiful*' in his poems. For all their wealth and depth of matter, they were without that naturalness, that absolute propriety of form which is essential to poetry. They were the products too exclusively of a profound thinker's attempts to get to the bottom of things, 'to *solve* the Universe', and too little of a genuine artist's desire to group things perfectly. They excited curiosity and reflection rather than pleasure. In fact, Clough was 'a mere d——d depth hunter'.

Not that Tennyson, a very different poet, was any better. In 1847 Arnold yawned at his dawdling with the painted shell of the Universe. Evidently a poet's true path was flanked by contrasting perils. On the one hand, there was the danger that he might with Clough achieve profundity at the price of failing in beauty; on the other, there was the danger that he might with Tennyson

achieve beauty of a kind by consenting to a trifling frag-
mentariness.

'*Not deep the poet sees, but wide*' ('Resignation'). His
true aim was to see life steadily and see it whole and,
thanks to this comprehensive vision, to achieve in his
work a perfect grouping of objects. Hence Arnold's
groan, 'For me you may often hear my sinews cracking
under the effort to unite matter. . . .' Hence, too, his
rueful admission, 'Composition, in the painter's sense—
that is the devil.'

The task was indeed especially difficult in the nineteenth century. In order to avoid a Tennysonian frag-
mentariness, the poet had to begin with 'an Idea of the
world . . . or . . . at least with isolated ideas'. If, however, in his search for such an Idea, he tried conscien-
tiously to take account of all that was known and thought
in so complex and disunited an age as his own, he might
only too easily lapse like Clough into earnest bewilderment and dispirited doubt. In such a frame of mind, he
might retain the sincerity requisite for verse like Clough's;
but he would very likely lose the creative ardour requisite
for poetry such as Arnold hoped to write.

Probably Arnold suspected that his own creative
ardour was not of the fiercest; and certainly he could not
claim to be himself exempt from the preoccupations,
doubts, and anxieties which so weighed upon Clough.
On the contrary, his first volume of poems was to show
him deeply affected by them. Nor was Clough the only
member of his set whom he saw plunging and bellowing in
the Time Stream. They were most of them, old Rugbeians
and others, strenuously engaged in solving the Universe.
If they had their way they would in the ordinary course
of friendship over-stimulate a similar activity in himself.
And might not that be the end of his poetic impulse?

By some means, they had to be kept at a slight distance; and Arnold's dandyism was the means chosen. Pococurantism, abhorred and denounced by the father, became to all appearances the son's creed. He flaunted a nonchalant indifference to the serious concerns of his associates. So much so that even as an undergraduate he had on one occasion to write in defence of his procedure:

> It is difficult for me to know in what terms to express myself after your last letter, so completely is it penetrated with that unfortunate error as to my want of interest in my friends which you say they have begun to attribute to me. It is an old subject which I need not discuss over again with you. The accusation, as you say, is not true. I laugh too much and they make one's laughter mean too much. However, the result is that when one wishes to be serious one cannot but fear a half suspicion on one's friends' parts that one is laughing, and, so, the difficulty gets worse and worse.

Five years later, during the Lansdowne House period, he was even more apprehensive of the threat to his creative spontaneity and assured himself with uncharacteristic harshness, 'Yes . . . something tells me I can, if need be, at last dispense with them all, even with him [*i.e.*, Clough]'. He subsequently admitted to Clough that at this time he had had a strong disposition to mental seclusion, and to the elimination of all influences which, he felt, troubled without advancing him; and he continued:

> You ask me in what I think or have thought you going wrong: in this: that you would never take your assiette as something determined final and unchangeable for you and proceed to work away on the basis of that: but were always poking and patching and cobbling at the assiette itself—could never finally, as it seemed—'resolve to be thyself'—but were looking for this and that experience, and doubting whether you

ought not to adopt this or that mode of being of persons
qui ne vous valaient pas because it might possibly be nearer
the truth than your own: you had no reason for thinking it
was, but it *might* be—and so you would try to adapt yourself
to it. You have I am convinced lost infinite time in this way:
it is what I call your morbid conscientiousness—you are the
most conscientious man I ever knew: but on some lines
morbidly so, and it spoils your action.

Late in the same year, 1853, he repeated the charge:
'You certainly do not seem to me sufficiently to desire
and earnestly strive towards—assured knowledge—
activity—happiness. You are too content to *fluctuate*—
to be ever learning, never coming to the knowledge of
the truth. This is why, with you, I feel it necessary to
stiffen myself—and hold fast my rudder.' Clough's own
recognition of this failing in himself is shown by his
allowing the Spirit to deride Dipsychus in such lines as:

> Methinks I see you,
> Through everlasting limbos of void time,
> Twirling and twiddling ineffectively,
> And indeterminately swaying for ever. (II, vi.)

On the other hand, Arnold's severity was that of one who
knew himself to be in some degree guilty of the offence
he was castigating but who was determined that if possible anxious speculation should not be allowed to sap
either his creative vitality as an artist or his strength of
purpose as a man.

So his friends had to bear with his dandyism. They
had to reconcile themselves to being addressed as in
this note which he wrote in 1850:

DEAR SLADE—I forgot to say last night that you must breakfast here to-morrow, Sunday, at 10 *pas plus tôt*, because John

Blackett is coming, who wishes to meet you. Ridiculous as such a desire is, it is too unimportant for me to refuse to gratify it.—Your faithful servant, M. ARNOLD.

Le Samedi matin.

The gaiety, impudence, and aloofness of this are all characteristic. But Clough, despite Arnold's fear of becoming infected with certain of his mental habits, was an altogether dearer and more intimate friend than the rest. When he was thinking of resigning his fellowship, Arnold was in his confidence; when he was about to leave for America, Arnold, having already helped him, made a warm offer of further financial assistance; and on receiving the news of his death Arnold wrote to his mother that it was 'a loss which I shall feel more and more as time goes on, for he is one of the few people who ever made a deep impression upon me'.

Naturally, Arnold kept Clough well informed during the eighteen-forties and the earlier eighteen-fifties regarding his own poetic hopes and aims. He protested to him against the view, too much fostered by the examples of Keats, Shelley, and Tennyson, and, before them, of 'those d——d Elizabethan poets generally', that the object of poetry was 'to produce exquisite bits and images'. On the contrary, said Arnold in 1852,

> modern poetry can only subsist by its *contents*: by becoming a complete magister vitae as the poetry of the ancients did: by including, as theirs did, religion with poetry, instead of existing as poetry only, and leaving religious wants to be supplied by the Christian religion, as a power existing independent of the poetical power. But the language, style and general proceedings of a poetry which has such an immense task to perform, must be very plain direct and severe: and it must not lose itself in parts and episodes and ornamental work, but must press forwards to the whole.

Not that he wished to elevate content at the expense of style. 'For the style is the expression of the nobility of the poet's character, as the matter is the expression of the richness of his mind: but on men character produces as great an effect as mind.'

His first volume, *The Strayed Reveller, and Other Poems*, was published at the beginning of 1849. Its contents surprised his sister Mary. They seemed like a new introduction to him. She found much more 'practical questioning' in the book than she had expected: 'in fact it showed a knowledge of life and conflict which was *strangely like experience* if it was not the thing itself; and this with all Matt's great power I should not have looked for.' In another letter she traced her surprise to the '*moral consciousness*' manifest in the poems, 'something which such a man as Clough has, for instance, which I did not expect to find in Matt; but it is there.'

This must have been a fairly representative reaction to the volume on the part of those acquaintances who had not had Clough's or Jane's opportunities of knowing what lay behind the eyeglass and the careless elegance of Lord Lansdowne's private secretary. But those who read it carefully must have found it an excellent preparation for Arnold's second volume, *Empedocles on Etna, and Other Poems*, which appeared in the autumn of 1852.

IV

On 29 September 1848, Arnold wrote to Clough from Switzerland, which he was visiting for perhaps the first time. 'Tomorrow I repass the Gemmi and get to Thun: linger one day at the Hotel Bellevue for the sake of the blue eyes of one of its inmates: and then proceed by slow stages down the Rhine to Cologne, thence to Amiens and Boulogne and England.' It may be that he had first met the possessor of these blue eyes during his previous Continental holiday in 1846–7. But there is no record of her at this earlier date. What his poems and letters make clear is that he saw her not only in 1848 but also when he revisited Thun almost exactly twelve months later; and that after 1849 there was no further reunion.

The lady's identity is unknown. The register of the Hotel Bellevue for the period in question has been destroyed; that of Thun Castle is also missing. The only available information about her is that contained in Arnold's poems and in the sentence already quoted from his holiday letter of 1848 to Clough. Both this letter and that which he wrote to Clough from Thun a year later are expressive of unusual emotional states. The former is almost exuberant, the latter sadly resolved.

In his volume of 1849, which was published during the interval between these two holidays, the lyric 'To my Friends, who ridiculed a tender Leave-taking' (later renamed 'A Memory-Picture') gave the lady the name, Marguerite, by which Arnold's readers were henceforward to know her and went on to describe her physical appearance. Combining this description with those given in the lyrical sequence 'Switzerland', of which certain items first appeared in the volume of 1852, it is possible to some extent to picture Marguerite. She had blue eyes; soft ash-coloured hair; a pale complexion; rounded cheeks; and a mouth which readily assumed an arch and mocking smile. She often wore a kerchief tied around her head. She moved with a 'pliant grace' and spoke in a clear, buoyant, and musical voice. She was French.

The setting for the love-affair is given with some fidelity in these poems. In one of them, the poet rides along the edge of the lake of Thun by moonlight, passes

the poplar avenue and 'the roof'd bridge that spans the
stream', the Aar, and hurries up the steep street towards
Marguerite's light. The Hotel Bellevue does in fact
stand in such a street as that to which these lines allude.
In other poems, Arnold refers to the great mountains of
the Oberland, which lie to the south, across the lake
from the old town.

These are the facts of the case, as far as they are known.
The temptation to supplement them with imaginings has
proved too strong for some biographers. One of these
believes that Marguerite was a governess, lady com-
panion, or teacher; another guesses that she was an
aristocrat; a third represents her as a Bohemian from
the Parisian theatre. Such conjectures destroy one
another.

Arnold's poems may not define Marguerite's social
and economic status; but they do make it possible to some
extent to trace the emotional graph of the relationship.
Is it not reasonable, for example, to guess that Marguerite's 'unconquer'd joy' was one of the things which
first attracted to her the young dandy who was striving
so hard not to succumb to the doubts and discourage-
ments which were infecting his friends? What is more
certain is that from the start Arnold was obsessed with
the notion that there was some insuperable obstacle in
the way of his continued acquaintance with Marguerite.
Even in the lyric which he published a half-year before
their last meeting, he admitted that

> Time's current strong
> Leaves us fixt to nothing long. ('A Memory-Picture.')

In those which he published after 1849, the power which
had finally separated him from her manifests itself as
'a God's tremendous voice', as a sea which rolls between

them, and as 'the darting river of Life' which bears him
away from her. It is impossible to say with complete
confidence what real or supposed impediment to their
union these metaphors hint at. But the poems themselves do suggest a partial explanation. The 'sea' which
'rolls between us' is said in 'Parting', the second of the
'Switzerland' series, to be 'Our different past'. The
poem continues:

> To the lips, ah! of others
> Those lips have been prest,
> And others, ere I was,
> Were strain'd to that breast;
>
> Far, far from each other
> Our spirits have grown.

In 'The Terrace at Berne', the last of the 'Switzerland'
poems to be written, this reference to Marguerite's past
life is echoed in Arnold's conjectures regarding her
existence since their parting ten years earlier. In fact,
Arnold seems to have believed that Marguerite was
sexually more experienced than himself; and that the
great difference between their past lives would quickly
force them apart.

On her side, Marguerite may well have been attracted
by the elegance and apparent self-possession of her
English admirer. She may even have seen him as a young
Milton on his travels! But before long his mournful
conviction that there was some insuperable barrier between them must, whether he expressed it openly to her
or not, have made him appear wavering and half-hearted.

> And women—things that live and move
> Mined by the fever of the soul—
> They seek to find in those they love
> Stern strength, and promise of control.
>
> ('A Farewell.')

So Marguerite broke with him. 'Absence' suggests that
he regained his emotional independence only slowly and
with difficulty.

This account is based exclusively upon those poems
in which there is explicit reference to Marguerite: 'A
Memory-Picture', 'A Dream', and the 'Switzerland'
series. It is possible that another eight or nine had their
emotional source in the love-affair. In the case of 'The
Forsaken Merman', this possibility becomes surely a
probability: the lady's name is Margaret, and the lovers
are separated by the uncompromising fact that they are
most at home in different physical elements. But it
would be foolhardy to build biography upon these doubtful instances.

Within nine or ten months of his last meeting with
Marguerite, Arnold was in the thick of another courtship. In a letter to Wyndham Slade, the recipient during
the previous year of the high-spirited invitation to breakfast already quoted, he wrote:

> Last night for the 5th time the deities interposed: I was
> asked specially to meet the young lady—my wheels burned
> the pavement—I mounted the stairs like a wounded quaggha,
> the pulsations of my heart shook all Park Crescent—my eyes
> devoured every countenance in the room in a moment of
> time: she was at the opera, and could not come. At the last
> moment her mother had had tickets sent her, and sent a
> note of excuse.
>
> I suffer from great dejection and lassitude this morning—
> having shown a Spartan fortitude on hearing the news last
> evening.

On 23 July 1850, Clough mentioned this elusive young
lady to Tom Arnold: 'Matt comes to Switzerland in a
month; after your sister's [*i.e.*, Jane's] wedding. He is
deep in a flirtation with Miss Wightman, daughter of the

Judge. It is thought it will come to something, for he has actually been to Church to meet her.' Despite Arnold's pertinacity, it seemed subsequently that the affair might come to nothing; for Sir William Wightman, a somewhat testy Scot, forbade the lovers to meet. Since Arnold's income as private secretary to Lord Lansdowne was not large, and since the Oriel fellowship was his only as long as he remained single, Wightman's objection to the match is comprehensible; and Arnold eventually did what he could to meet it.

Meanwhile, Frances Lucy Wightman and her father were setting off on a Continental holiday. Arnold's 'Calais Sands', the first draft of which was apparently posted to the lady, tells how, 'Mixt with the idlers on the pier', he gave himself the pleasure of witnessing her arrival in France, without, however, presuming to show himself; and it concludes with his determination to spend that night in the same hotel as the Wightmans. On the following day, he left. 'On the Rhine', the fourth of the five lyrics composing the sequence 'Faded Leaves', was evidently written during the next stage of a tour which was taking him once again to 'the high Alps'. 'Faded Leaves' is concerned throughout with his love for Frances Wightman.

Soon after his return to England, Arnold began to look about him for a more stable and remunerative form of employment, such as would permit him to renew his courtship. On the advice of William Ralph Lingen, who had been his tutor at Balliol and who was by this time Secretary to the Committee of the Council on Education, he turned his thoughts to an Inspectorship of Schools. Lord Lansdowne, as President of the Council, was the nominal head of the Department of Education, and on 14 April 1851 he made Arnold an Inspector. Wightman's

consent to the marriage had been obtained a fortnight
earlier, presumably in anticipation of this appointment.
The wedding took place on 10 June 1851, and the honeymoon was spent in France, Switzerland, and Italy.

'You'll like my Lucy; she has all my sweetness and
none of my airs!' said Arnold, with characteristic impudence, to one of his old Oxford friends. Fanny Lucy, or
Flu, was, indeed, very generally liked. The Arnold family
took to her. Old Crabb Robinson, who met the couple
at Fox How during the autumn of the year following the
marriage, was favourably impressed. Clough wrote to
his fiancée, 'I like the wife very well,—more, the more
I see of her'. In 'Faded Leaves' there are a few references
to her physical appearance as a young woman. The poet
speaks of her brown hair and her grey eyes, or, rather, her

> Eyes too expressive to be blue,
> Too lovely to be grey. ('On the Rhine.')

In the first poem of the sequence, her 'mocking mouth'
reminds the reader of Marguerite's. Did both ladies find
that their suitor's affectations invited teasing?

Matthew and his wife had six children, four boys and
two girls. One boy, Richard, and the two girls, Lucy
and Eleanor, reached adult life. Of the other three boys,
Basil died in infancy, Thomas and Trevenen ('Budge') in
their teens. Despite these bereavements, it was a remarkably happy marriage. Both husband and wife were
extremely sociable and kept in touch with a wide circle
of friends. Fanny Lucy also shared Matthew's love of
travel; and he found that her company was essential to
his fullest enjoyment of it. Tom had indeed been mistaken when, during his brother's engagement, he had
described him as one of the very last men in the world
to be happy in matrimony.

V

Arnold spent the greater part of his active life in an occupation, school-inspection, which seemed to have little connection with his serious literary endeavours. His wish to marry, and that alone, induced him to enter it; he approached it without enthusiasm, and to the end he disliked the routine work which it entailed. At first he dreamed of an early retirement to Italy or of a diplomatic appointment in Switzerland. Knowing that foreign life was thoroughly congenial to him 'and *liberating* in the highest degree', he longed to withdraw with his wife and children and to devote himself, probably among the Alps, to writing. But by the opening months of 1859 he was convinced that this longing was simply irresponsible. 'I shall work best in the long-run by living in the country which is my own.'

Living there did not necessarily mean grinding away as a school-inspector, however. In 1866, in 1867, and yet again in 1869, he had hopes of obtaining more agreeable employment. On each occasion he was disappointed. After his promotion to a Senior Inspectorship in 1870, he seems to have given up all thought of a change. In 1884, two years before his retirement, he became a Chief Inspector.

During the nineteenth century, the state accepted no responsibility for secondary education. So Arnold, for the thirty-five years of his service, was concerned in the ordinary course of his duty solely with primary, or elementary, schools and with training colleges for primary-school teachers. Until 1871, moreover, only inspectors in Anglican orders were appointed for Church of England schools. So Arnold, during the first twenty

D

years of his career, was restricted to establishments under mainly Nonconformist control. In his dealings with these and with their managers, he acquired the familiarity with British middle-class life in some of its most characteristic manifestations, which helped to make him eventually so formidable a critic of it.

At first, his inspectorial district was very large. It stretched from the North Sea to Cardigan Bay and included the English midlands and practically the whole of Wales. For some years, in consequence, his life was one of almost incessant travelling; and he made it even more nomadic by acting as Marshal when his father-in-law went on official tours as a Judge. Arnold could enjoy travelling. But this was travelling at its worst and in association with work which he found tedious and depressing. A bad carriage on a filthy line; a bun snatched hastily in a railway station; thirty pupil teachers to examine in an inconvenient room, and nothing to eat except a biscuit given by a charitable lady; eighty training-college candidates to supervise for seven hours a day, with the gas burning most of the time 'either to give light or to help warm the room'—these were the conditions of which Arnold spoke in his letters and in which he had to seize what time he could for his poetry. 'I did not arrive here till just two, as the train was late; went to the school, and found there were three of them. About four o'clock I found myself so exhausted, having eaten nothing since breakfast, that I sent out for a bun, and ate it before the astonished school.' So he wrote of a visit made a few months before his *Poems* of 1853 appeared. On this particular occasion, things improved. 'Since then I have had a very good extempore dinner on mutton chops and bread pudding, all the Quaker household having dined early, and now'—an unwelcome prospect after the warm hospitality—'I am in for the pupil teachers till ten o'clock.' There can have been little poetry on this day, unless he made use of that morning train-journey. And how remote both the rue de Rivoli and the Alps must have seemed!

So restless was his life that it was not until 1858 that he was able to give his wife a settled home away from her parents. He wrote to a friend: 'We have taken a house in Chester Square. It is a very small one, but it will be something to unpack one's portmanteau for the first time since I was married, now nearly seven years ago.' Fortunately, his district had not remained as large as at first. Already, by 1858, it had been reduced to a more compact group of counties, most of them in the south-east; and it was eventually narrowed to the neighbourhood of London itself.

Although he now spent less of his life on the railway, Arnold still disliked the routine of inspecting and examining. But he never doubted the importance of educational work. He was himself the son of a great schoolmaster. He saw clearly that it was upon the teachers in the state-aided primary schools that the task would devolve of 'civilising the next generation of the lower classes, who, as things are going, will have most of the political power of the country in their hands'. He wrote these words in 1851, shortly after taking up his appointment. Later, he defined 'civilisation' as 'the humanisation of man in society'. This, and not mere instruction, was, he believed, the true aim of all education, the aim by reference to which alone the success of teachers, curricula, and administrative schemes could be estimated. Accordingly, he wrote again and again in his notes after visiting schools of which he approved: 'the children human'.

Arnold was not afraid to make education, so conceived, a responsibility of the state. In this he was following his own father and Coleridge and Burke in their insistence that the state had the positive duty of humanizing and civilizing its members. By the same token, he was defying the revered principle of *laissez-faire*. In the very year in which he became an inspector, the *Economist* denounced grants of public money in aid of schools as 'bounties on a species of production [an educated populace!] not at the moment in demand'. Ruskin's mockery of 'the divine principle of demand and supply' was assuredly called for and must in due course have been read with some sympathy by Arnold. Certainly, he advocated an extension of state influence. He wished to see good schools of various grades and types established throughout the country; and he wished these schools to be the constituent parts of a coherent national system of education. While adhering to the principle of fee-paying, he maintained that attendance should be made compulsory at the primary grade.

In any primary school which was sincerely dedicated to the humanization of man in society, religious instruction would, he thought, be an integral part of the work. English, too, would be central if the school aspired to be genuinely 'formative and *humanising*'. French, in addition to its commercial utility, possessed a great cultural value; and Latin might profitably be taught to a few picked, older pupils. On the other side, Arnold went so far as to advocate the introduction of natural science as a compulsory subject in primary schools; but he insisted upon its subordination to the humanities.

To have the power of using . . . [the] data of natural science, a man must, in general, have first been in some measure *moralised*; and for moralising him it will be found not easy,

I think, to dispense with those old agents, letters, poetry, religion. So let not our teachers be led to imagine, whatever they may hear and see of the call for natural science, that their literary cultivation is unimportant. The fruitful use of natural science itself depends, in a very great degree, on having effected in the whole man, by means of letters, a rise in what the political economists call *the standard of life*. ('General Report for 1876.')

To one who held such views as these, the Revised Code of 1862 was sadly retrogressive. According to this, two-thirds of the grant payable to a primary school was to depend upon the individual examination of its children in reading, writing, and arithmetic, and only one-third upon the number of them attending satisfactorily. This system of payment mainly according to the results obtained in the teaching of the three R's seemed to Arnold to couple a lowering of educational standards with what he derisively labelled 'a *prize scheme*'. He held that a grant ought to be 'given to a school not as a mere machine for teaching reading, writing, and arithmetic, but as a living whole with complex functions, religious, moral, and intellectual'.

By his pen, Arnold contributed notably to the defeat of the initial intention that grants should be entirely dependent upon the performances of the pupils in the three prescribed subjects. But his continued opposition did not prevent the system of 'payment by results' in its modified form from surviving him. At first he wondered whether his writing against the Revised Code might jeopardize his position in the Department of Education. 'I don't think, however, they can eject me,' he wrote to his wife, 'though they can, and perhaps will, make my place uncomfortable. If thrown on the world I daresay we should be on our legs again before very long. Any

way, I think I owed as much as this to a cause in which
I have now a deep interest, and always shall have, even
if I cease to serve it officially.' But his brother-in-law,
William Forster, was rightly of opinion that the authorities could not touch him and would bring a storm on their
heads if they tried; and, after the Code had been modified,
Lingen, the Secretary, and his wife attended a dinner-
party at the Arnolds' and were very amiable.

Arnold felt, and said, that the new regulations inevitably gave both to teaching and to inspection a mechanical
turn which could only tend to stultify the intellectual life
of the schools. He evidently strove in his own official
visits to be as little as possible a mere registering clerk,
as was required by the new system, and as much as
possible a sympathetic supervisor, as had been required
by the old. In consequence, a more orthodox colleague
could cast doubt on his efficiency as an instrument of the
Revised Code and could tell a no doubt exaggerated story
about his method of inspection. According to this, a
London school manager had said, 'Mr. Arnold inspects
our school in Westminster. . . . Of course we are
much honoured, and the managers make a point of
attending to meet him. He arrives in the course of the
morning; shakes hands with the managers and teachers;
and talks very pleasantly for a few minutes; then he
walks through the classes between the desks, looking
over the children's shoulders at some exercises, and so
makes his way to the door, and we see him no more.'
Evidently the elegant insouciance of Lord Lansdowne's
private secretary mellowed into this urbane casualness
of the middle-aged inspector. Though he could no
longer be thought idle, he could at least assert, 'No one
shall say that I am a punctual Inspector.' He still carried
an eyeglass. And he was still capable of the old playful

impertinence. When inspecting schools in Edmonton, he preferred not to remain overnight in that town but to travel there daily from his home. A heavy claim for expenses resulted, in response to which he received an official note: 'Mr. M. Arnold, H.M.I. Why not stay at Edmonton?' 'How can you expect me to stay at Edmonton,' he retorted, 'when John Gilpin couldn't?' His claim was allowed.

Despite his nonchalance, and despite his dislike of routine work, his inspecting was effective in precisely those ways which he himself rightly considered most important. According to a contemporary, 'He became the teachers' and children's friend, and though many a droll anecdote of his casual methods of marking and taking stock of his schools still goes the rounds, . . . none of his colleagues had a shrewder sense of what was wanting in each school he visited, or could reckon it up more readily. For the general body of elementary teachers he thus acquired an honest respect and liking.' His assistant inspector described him as having inspired many young teachers to the study of literature and to the undertaking of London degrees for their own improvement, and the eventual benefit of their pupils. Another younger colleague held that, 'indirectly, his fine taste, his gracious and kindly manner, his honest and generous recognition of any new form of excellence which he observed, all tended to raise the aims and tone of the teachers with whom he came in contact, and to encourage in them self-respect and respect for their work'. He had little to do with arranging the minutiae of educational administration, but, 'when questions of principle were involved, he was frequently consulted, and we who were his colleagues received from him at times very weighty and practical suggestions'. Even a

teacher who was writing to defend his school against a
severe report of Arnold's felt obliged to add, in a letter
which Arnold was not meant to see, that he had not a
word against the inspector, whom he would rather have
than any other he had ever come in contact with, 'as he
was always gentle and patient with the children'. The
letter came to Arnold's notice, and he was naturally
very gratified. Writing to his mother, he commented,
'The great thing is *humanity*, after all.'

Three times he was sent on special missions to the
Continent. In 1859, he toured France, Holland, and
Switzerland inspecting primary schools for the Newcastle
Commission; in 1865, he went to France, Italy, Germany
Austria, and Switzerland to report on secondary schools
and universities for a Schools Inquiry Commission; and
in 1885–6, immediately before his retirement, he inves-
tigated the German, Swiss, and French systems of free
schools on behalf of his office. Much as he disliked any
prolonged separation from his family, he rejoiced in
these opportunities for extensive travel. In the autumn
of 1865 he wrote, after spending six months on the
Continent, 'I feel as if I should never want again to
come abroad for those little six-week rushes which the
English are so fond of, and which I once used to think
the height of felicity.'

The six months in question constituted the only period
during which he was officially concerned with secondary
education. Nevertheless, he attached the greatest importance to the organization and improvement of those
institutions to which, in the existing circumstances, the
middle class, and that alone, owed such education as it
received. This class was for the moment supreme. But
its schooling in dismal academies like the tyrannical Mr.
Creakle's Salem House, where David Copperfield suffered,

could not be said to have fitted it for its responsibilities.
If the middle class was worthily to discharge the functions
which it had inherited from an aristocracy whose day
was over, it was essential that it should be truly civilized
in schools which had been brought into an effective connection with the state. Arnold therefore repeatedly
urged his contemporaries to organize their secondary
education; and, since it was desirable that some sort of
university training should be available to the middle class,
he recommended them to organize their higher education, too. His purpose in this was, as always, the
humanization of man in society—the humanization, in
this instance, of the puritanical middle class. The thought
of the bad civilization of this class was, he said, the
master-thought by which his politics were governed.

VI

Shortly after the publication of the *Poems* of 1853, an
old Oxford friend wrote to Tom, who was out of the
country, that Matt was 'greatly improved by his marriage
—retaining all the genius and nobleness of mind which
you remember, with all the lesser faults pruned and
softened down'. Responsibilities, both domestic and
professional, were certainly disciplining the exuberance
which could so disconcert his acquaintances. Moreover,
he was feeling keenly the loss of his youth.

Admittedly, he was only entering his thirties. But
the early Victorian period was one in which it was
possible for a now forgotten poetaster of twenty-seven,
contributing to a popular annual, to describe himself as
on the verge of middle age and to vow that henceforth
his muse should be the bride of heaven! Arnold was
relatively moderate. He was very nearly twenty-nine

when he wrote to Clough: 'we are growing old, and advancing towards the deviceless darkness: it would be well not to reach it till we had at least tried *some* of the things men consider desirable'. Four months later, he exclaimed to the same friend, 'How life rushes away, and youth. One has dawdled and scrupled and fiddle faddled —and it is all over.' True, this is a theme on which any correspondent might have been tempted to dwell in letters to one who had dawdled and scrupled and fiddle-faddled as much as Clough. But Arnold touched on it also in letters to Jane, though with a significant shift of emphasis. Five months before his marriage, he lamented to her that a man's commitment of himself to his particular course in life involved the renunciation of many other courses which had lain invitingly open to him in youth. As a result, he said, one grew up 'shorn of so many beams'. Late in 1853, he remarked to her 'how the cares of life deepen about one' after thirty. His sense of constriction was such that in the same year he confessed to Clough, 'I am past thirty, and three parts iced over'.

Ten years later, he had very largely adjusted himself to his responsibilities. At times, he could still feel that he was getting old amidst a press of occupations for which he had not been born. 'I must go back to my charming occupation of hearing students give lessons. Here is my programme for this afternoon: Avalanches – The Steam Engine – The Thames – India Rubber – Bricks – The Battle of Poictiers – Subtraction – The Reindeer – The Gunpowder Plot – The Jordan. Alluring, is it not? Twenty minutes each, and the days of one's life are only threescore years and ten.' But no one outside his most intimate circle ever heard him complain of the drudgery of his life. For years he had been making an habitual war

on depression and low spirits. Moreover, he could feel
that he was still slowly ripening; and he could wonder
whether he would continue to feel so to the end. Having
written very little verse in recent years, he resolved in
1861 to discontinue his critical writing for the time being
and to dedicate his forties to poetry. 'It is my last chance.
It is not a bad ten years of one's life for poetry if one
resolutely uses it, but it is a time in which, if one does
not use it, one dries up and becomes prosaic altogether.'

Poetry, however, was to employ very little of his
time. Most of the volume, *New Poems*, which he published
in 1867 had been written many years earlier; and after
1867 he practically ceased to write verse. But he had
not been mistaken when he had spoken of himself as
still ripening and as possessing an increasingly strong
sense of purpose. What he had not suspected was the
extent to which this purpose would fulfil itself in prose.

His first critical essay had been the 'Preface' to his
Poems of 1853. Only when he was elected to the Professorship of Poetry at Oxford four years later did he,
in preparing his lectures, begin to write literary criticism
regularly. This post, which he held for the full permitted
period of ten years, entailed only light duties such as he
could perform in addition to his school inspection.
Principally, he had to deliver three lectures each year.
He was the first layman to occupy the chair and the first
Professor to speak from it in English instead of Latin.
As a lecturer, he was not outstanding, though he achieved
some successes; and he derived little stimulus from his
'wooden' Oxford audiences. In preparing his material,
he had to think not of the 'dead bones' who would come
to hear him but of the public which would subsequently
read him. Otherwise, he said, his spirit would have
failed. When he relinquished the Professorship in 1867,

he continued to address this wider public in prose criticism.

His acknowledged master was the great French critic Charles Augustin Sainte-Beuve, whose work he had admired since the Lansdowne House period. He sent to Sainte-Beuve copies of many of his publications from the *Poems* of 1853 onwards; and Sainte-Beuve inserted a translation of the 'Stanzas in Memory of the Author of *Obermann*' into his *Chateaubriand et son Groupe Littéraire sous l'Empire* (1860) and both in that work and elsewhere made respectful mention of his disciple. The two men met in Paris during the hot August of 1859, while Arnold was on the first of his inspectorial visits to the Continent. They dined at the Restaurant Pinson, returned to Sainte-Beuve's house for tea, and talked until midnight. Arnold walked back to his hotel but slept badly. His excitement was still evident when he described the meeting to his wife two days later. Further meetings occurred during his second official tour in 1865.

To Arnold, Sainte-Beuve was 'the first of living critics', an estimate avowed not only in letters to his mother and to Sainte-Beuve himself but also in published utterances. The flexibility, the delicacy, and the disinterested curiosity of the French critic had earned him this position; and Arnold, as has been seen, was later to bracket him with Goethe, Wordsworth, and Newman as one of the four men from whom he had learned 'habits, methods, ruling ideas'.

Shortly after Sainte-Beuve's death in 1869, Arnold contributed an obituary notice to an English periodical. In this he alluded to the poetry and the single novel which Sainte-Beuve had written as a young man and recognized that, despite the shortcomings of this creative work, 'his preference, his dream, his ideal' had been there, and that for him criticism had been labour of an inferior kind. But, said Arnold, Sainte-Beuve was a first-rate critic; and 'first-rate criticism has a permanent value greater than that of any but first-rate works of poetry and art'. It seems likely that in writing these words Arnold was thinking not only of his friend's case but also of his own.

He had by this date published three volumes of literary criticism: *On Translating Homer* (1861), *Essays in Criticism* (1865), and *On the Study of Celtic Literature* (1867). These had been followed by *Culture and Anarchy* (1869), the first of a number of works exemplifying his belief that the disinterested intelligence of the literary critic had an essential task to perform in fields generally thought to require the application of specialist techniques. In *Culture and Anarchy* and in the lighter *Friendship's Garland* (1871), he handled social and political problems; in *St. Paul and Protestantism* (1870), *Literature and Dogma* (1873), *God and the Bible* (1875), and *Last Essays on Church and Religion* (1877), he grappled with the question of religious belief. The sixties and seventies saw also the publication of several of his works on education and concluded with the appearance of a collection of political and literary studies entitled *Mixed Essays* (1879).

These works provoked a good deal of opposition. But Arnold was able to feel, from about 1868 onwards, that what he wrote as a critic was beginning to tell and that it was the more effective for his determination to preserve always an easy, good-humoured, urbane tone. He was right when he claimed in 1871 that John Morley had learned something from him, and knew it; and Morley was by no means his only disciple among the younger men. Nevertheless, Arnold was still not a popular writer. He said as much, though in rather special

circumstances, when late in 1870 he appealed to the Income Tax Commissioners against their assessment of his
profits as a man of letters at £1,000 a year. (This was as
much as he earned by his inspecting.) 'You see before you,
gentlemen,' he said, 'what you have often heard of, *an
unpopular author*.' When the assessment was cut down to
£200 a year, he told them that he would have to write
more articles in order to prevent his being a loser by
submitting even to this. 'Then the public', said the
chairman politely, 'will have reason to be much obliged
to us.'

Literature and Dogma, which appeared nearly three
years later, was his first best-seller. Arnold derived much
satisfaction from this wider dissemination of his influence.
His self-assured manner was no longer a protective disguise; it was now the natural manner of one whose
'*Werther* period' was well behind him. This period, says
Goethe, belongs 'to the career of every individual who,
with an innate free natural instinct, must accommodate
himself to the narrow limits of an antiquated world.
Obstructed fortune, restrained activity, unfulfilled wishes,
are the calamities . . . of every individual man; and it
would be bad indeed if everybody had not, once in his
life, known a time when *Werther* seemed as if it had been
written for him alone.' Arnold's poetry had been largely
the product of his *Werther* period; but his criticism came
from a well-adjusted, and eventually well-established,
man of letters.

He mixed freely in London society. Once at least, he
accepted no fewer than five dinner-invitations for a single
week. At his club, the Athenaeum, he knew 'something
resembling beatitude'. Admittedly, this was due partly
to the excellent library; but he valued the social ameni-
ties, too. His relative and friend, T. H. Huxley, the

scientist and agnostic, was a member; so was his mother's friend, Crabb Robinson, who complimented him there early in 1867 on his great reputation and was stimulated by the ensuing conversation to take up *Essays in Criticism*, probably the last book the old man read. On one occasion members were amused to see their radical theologian engaged in talk with a brace of bishops; and on another it was Disraeli, the conservative Prime Minister, whom Arnold greeted as he entered. He knew most of the leading writers of the day. Tennyson enjoyed what he called 'Mat's sublime waggery'; and Arnold had a particularly warm regard for Robert Browning, whom he would gladly have seen as his successor in the Chair of Poetry at Oxford.

During these middle years, Arnold was welcomed to many of the country houses of the aristocracy, the great fortified posts of the Barbarians as he laughingly termed them. He frequently visited Aston Clinton in Buckinghamshire, where he had an intimate friend and an understanding reader in Louisa, the wife of Sir Anthony de Rothschild. A poor shot, he himself said that he participated in the sports of the Barbarians in vain. But he enjoyed fishing and walking and skating. For their physically bracing effect, he especially valued his drill-nights with the Queen's Westminster Rifle Volunteers. As for games, he played some croquet, grew very fond of billiards, and occasionally watched cricket.

In 1868 he and his family moved to Harrow, where the three sons were to be educated. Byron House, their new home, was well-built and roomy and had a large and attractive garden. Here Prince Thomas of Savoy, the young Duke of Genoa, was their guest while in attendance at the school. At the conclusion of his stay, his father, the King of Italy, honoured Arnold by the award of a decoration. Here, too, Arnold lost the two sons who died in their teens. As a result of these bereavements, the family moved in 1873 into a smaller house, Pains Hill Cottage, at Cobham, Surrey, within a few miles of Laleham. This was Arnold's home for the rest of his life. The daughter of his brother Tom who eventually became well known as Mrs. Humphry Ward liked in her old age to look back upon her visits here:

> . . . our expeditions to Cobham where he lived, in the pretty cottage beside the Mole [the stream which runs by Cobham], are marked in memory with a very white stone. The only drawback to the Cobham visits were the 'dear, dear boys'! —i.e. the dachshunds, Max and Geist, who, however adorable in themselves, had no taste for visitors and no intention of letting such intruding creatures interfere with their possession of their master. One would go down to Cobham, eager to talk to 'Uncle Matt' about a book or an article— covetous at any rate of *some* talk with him undisturbed. And it would all end in a breathless chase after Max, through field after field where the little wretch was harrying either sheep or cows, with the dear poet, hoarse with shouting, at his heels. The dogs were always *in the party*, talked to, caressed, or scolded exactly like spoilt children; and the cat of the house was almost equally dear. Once, at Harrow, the then ruling cat—a tom—broke his leg, and the house was in lamentation. The vet. was called in, and hurt him horribly. Then Uncle Matt ran up to town, met Professor Huxley at the Athenaeum, and anxiously consulted him. 'I'll go down with you,' said Huxley. The two travelled back instanter to Harrow, and while Uncle Matt held the cat, Huxley—who had begun life, let it be remembered, as Surgeon to the *Rattlesnake*!—examined him, the two black heads together. There is a rumour that Charles Kingsley was included in the consultation. Finally the limb was put in splints, and left to nature. All went well. (*A Writer's Recollections*, pp. 241–2.)

Arnold was particularly happy in his family life. His letters contain many fond records of his children's words and deeds. Dick and Lucy shared their parents' love of travel, Dick[1] and his invalid brother Tom their mother's taste for music. (This taste was as deficient in Matthew, who could speak of going to *see* a Wagner opera, as in his favourite sister, Jane.) Like his father, Dick took readily to fishing. Again like his father, he caused anxiety at home by his idleness at Oxford. He was reading history; and Matthew formed the lowest opinion of the course: 'nothing but read, read, read, endless histories in English, many of them by quite second-rate men; nothing to form the mind as reading truly great authors forms it, or even to exercise it as learning a new language, or mathematics, or one of the natural sciences exercises it'. Heavy debts incurred by Dick at Oxford were the ultimate cause of his father's later needing to make a large profit from his lecture-tour in the United States.

With the gradual settlement of his thought during the eighteen-sixties, Arnold became more and more aware that in his social and religious criticism he was conspicuously his father's son, 'and his continuator'. This realization seems to have given him additional confidence as he strove to charm and to convert 'the wild beast of Philistinism''—in other words, persuasively to correct the 'self-assertion and narrowness' of the British middle class. His sense of this purpose, and of his opportunity to fulfil it, was strong enough to keep him eager and sanguine despite increasing years; and his letters and note-books show how rigorously he tried to plan his time to the best advantage. He had, indeed, emerged from his *Werther* period.

[1] He was later the 'R.P.A.' of Sir Edward Elgar's *Enigma Variations*.

E

VII

A lady who met Arnold at a party in London about eight years before his death was impressed by his humorous vivacity and affectionate kindliness. He was taking an almost boyish delight in being with some of his old college friends again. His hair was thick and black, while theirs had become thin and grey; and suspecting that one of them was staring at him Arnold exclaimed, 'Ah, Sandars, you are jealous! You think it is a wig! But pull it, Sandars, pull it!' His hair was indeed a 'perpetual miracle'; the only grey hairs he could claim were 'internal'.

His kindliness, geniality, and courtesy were widely acknowledged. Years later, a friend in Anglican orders wrote: 'One of his pleasantest characteristics was his perfect readiness to discuss, with complete command of temper, views and opinions of his own, which he knew I did not share, and thought dangerous. Many and many a conversation have I had with him at the Athenaeum, and never did an unkindly or peevish word fall from him.' This was echoed by another friend who spoke of his great charm and his having been a delightful man to argue with, 'even though he could be very patronising. But there was in all he said a kind of understood though seldom expressed sadness, as if to say, "It will soon be all over, don't let us get angry; we are all very good fellows," etc.'

During his last years, Arnold continued to lead an active social life. In 1880 he accepted an invitation from the Duchess of Norfolk to meet Newman; the two men had corresponded some years earlier, and Arnold had gracefully acknowledged that Newman was one of his masters. At this first and last meeting, the old man took Arnold's hand in both of his and said, 'I ventured to tell the Duchess I should like to see you.' At a party in London early in the following year, Arnold had a long talk with Disraeli, who at this last of a number of encounters scattered over several decades congratulated him on being 'the only living Englishman who had become a classic in his own lifetime'. Arnold understood this to refer to his successful launching of nicknames and catch-phrases such as 'Philistine' and 'sweetness and light'. Certainly these were widely current—so much so that as early as 1870 the Chancellor of the University of Oxford had said after conferring an honorary degree on Arnold that he ought perhaps to have addressed him as the sweetest and most lucid of men, *Vir dulcissime et lucidissime*!

During these last years, as always, Arnold travelled extensively in his own country and abroad both on duty and for pleasure. Whenever possible, he was accompanied by members of his family. His wife and his elder daughter Lucy were with him on his first visit to the United States, a lecture-tour, in 1883–4. Arnold's first glimpse of the New World showed him 'a beautiful *orné* landscape with spires, villas, hills, and woods'. 'Just like Richmond,' he remarked to someone on deck near him, 'and not a single Mohican running about!' This comment found its way into the American newspapers.

While it would be unfair to suggest that these were uniformly discourteous to the visitor, they certainly gave Arnold ample reason for disliking and eventually despising them. One of them published an impertinent description of him: 'He has harsh features, supercilious manners, parts his hair down the middle, wears a single eye-glass and ill-fitting clothes.' Shortly after his arrival, the

Chicago *Tribune* attacked him violently for lecturing for 'filthy lucre'; after his departure, when a rival hoaxed it into ferociously denouncing him for an alleged severe criticism of Chicago and its people, the *Tribune* reported Arnold's denial of his authorship under the headlines: 'Arnold denies; Mr. Medill [the editor and supposedly Arnold's friend] refuses to accept Arnold's disclaimer; says Arnold is a cur.' Naturally enough, Arnold came to think the newspapers the worst feature of American life.

Occasionally they amused him. There was, for example, the comparison of himself, as he stooped now and then during a lecture to look at his manuscript, to 'an elderly bird pecking at grapes on a trellis'.

His first lecture, given in New York in a larger hall than he had ever used before, was unsuccessful. People were unable to hear him and left; among them was General Grant, the great military hero of the Civil War, who said, 'Well, wife, we have paid to see the British lion; we cannot hear him roar, so we had better go home.' Two brief periods of coaching by an Andover theological professor helped him to make himself more audible, and his tour, despite some resistance in the Mid-west, proved a very fair success. Everywhere, he was deeply gratified by the kindness of his hosts. One of these was the old showman, Phineas Barnum. He had sent an invitation: 'You, Mr. Arnold, are a celebrity, I am a notoriety; we ought to be acquainted.' Arnold had agreed and had become his guest. Barnum heard the lecture, 'Numbers', in which Arnold distinguished between the majority in any society and that 'remnant' which leavens the lump. He thought it 'grand' and resolved, he told Arnold, to belong to the remnant.

Before the tour was half over, Lucy detached herself from the '*Matthew Arnold troupe*' (as the party was called

on the special theatrical railway tickets issued to it).
She greatly enjoyed a long stay in New York and there
became engaged to the American whom she later married. Her first daughter was the Arnolds' first grand-
child and the immediate occasion of their second visit
to America—this time with their younger daughter, the
brown-haired Eleanor, or Nelly—in 1886. Following
this visit, Arnold summarized his impressions in an
essay entitled 'Civilization in the United States'. He had
found much to admire in American political institutions;
his belief in the value of social equality had been confirmed by his experience of American life; but he had
to insist that that life was grievously lacking in beauty
and distinction.

The year 1886 was also his last year as an inspector of
schools. In 1883 he had been greatly surprised when
Gladstone, whom he had supposed hostile to him, had
offered him a Civil list pension of £250 a year, 'as a
public recognition of service to the poetry and literature
of England'. At first it had seemed to Arnold that a man
who was already drawing a substantial income from the
public purse could not be justified in accepting such an
offer; but his friends Morley and Lingen had urged him
to take it. By persuading him to do so, they had greatly
facilitated his retirement.

This was not to be the retirement to Italy of which he
had once dreamed. Despite his lifelong attachment to
Oxford, he thought Florence the most beautiful place
he knew. But he could not uproot himself from his
beloved cottage and garden at Cobham. There he spent
most of his last eighteen months. During this time, he
paid several visits: to his unmarried sister at Fox How,
for example, and to the de Rothschilds at Aston Clinton.
But in the main he lived quietly at home in Surrey.

Quiet was obligatory. In the spring of 1885 he had begun to suffer from a pain across his chest. 'I feel very unlike lawn tennis,' he had written to Dick, now married and living in Manchester, 'as going fast or going up hill gives me the sense of having a mountain on my chest; luckily, in fishing, one goes slow and stands still a good deal.' He had been mortified to find himself stopping half a dozen times in going up to Pains Hill. 'But so', he had reflected, 'one draws to one's end.' An optimistic diagnosis of indigestion had evidently left him sceptical.

By August, however, things had improved sufficiently for him to walk and to play lawn tennis as Lord Aberdare's guest while attending the Welsh national Eisteddfod. During the following winter, he had suffered little in-convenience on his last inspectorial visit to the Continent; and while spending Christmas at home he had skated. But the pain had returned more violently during his visit to America in the summer of 1886. He had found the climate trying; and a tumble while sea-bathing had intro-duced a week of particularly troublesome attacks. Lucy had been very good to him; but he could not seriously think of crossing the Atlantic on a third visit.

Back at Cobham, he soon felt restored. 'If I go too quick, I am stopped by a warning in my chest, but I can go about as much as I like if I go leisurely, and I have no attacks of sharp pain.' By this time he had certainly recognized the symptoms of *angina pectoris*, which had killed both his father and his grandfather. No doubt his busy and nomadic life had aggravated the condition. So he lived quietly, reading, writing, watching his garden, botanizing, playing tenderly with his domestic pets, and enjoying the company of his relatives and friends. During the winter of 1886–7 he skated once more; and there is surely disappointment in a remark of the following winter, 'the lake is all frozen, but the ice is rotten'.

The end came very suddenly. In 1888 Lucy and her daughter were expected in England. Arnold went from Cobham to Liverpool, where they were to land. On the afternoon of the next day, 15 April, overjoyed at the thought of soon meeting them, he leaped lightheartedly over a low fence while running for a tram and at once dropped dead. He was sixty-five years of age.

THE POET

I

Of the volumes of poetry which Arnold published before he was forty-five, six contain substantial quantities of new work; and there is very little of his verse which is not to be found in one or another of these six collections. The earliest of them have already been named: *The Strayed Reveller, and Other Poems* (1849) and *Empedocles on Etna, and Other Poems* (1852). These 'other poems' include many well-known works. 'Resignation', 'The Forsaken Merman', and the sonnet 'Shakespeare' belong to the earlier volume, and 'Memorial Verses', 'A Summer Night', 'Stanzas in Memory of the Author of *Obermann*', and most of the love poems to the later one. Both volumes were withdrawn as soon as Arnold had transferred to his *Poems* of 1853 as many of their contents as he wished at that date to preserve. The new poems in this third collection include 'Sohrab and Rustum', 'Philomela', 'Requiescat', and 'The Scholar-Gipsy'. *Poems: Second Series* (1855) opens with 'Balder Dead'; otherwise, it contains only one short poem not salvaged from one or other of the two earliest volumes. *Merope*, a tragedy on the Greek model, followed in 1858, being calculated, as Arnold somewhat uninvitingly told a correspondent, 'rather to inaugurate my Professorship with dignity than to move deeply the present race of *humans*'. Finally, *New Poems* (1867) contained still further salvage from the volume of 1852—notably 'Empedocles on Etna' itself—and, among its genuinely new poems,

'Thyrsis', 'Dover Beach', 'Palladium', 'Growing Old', and 'Obermann Once More'. Of the new poems, several had certainly been written many years earlier; three had been printed in periodicals—only one of them recently —and a fourth in an anthology. It is clear that Arnold had not written a great deal of verse since 1855; and he was to produce only seven poems more, three of them elegies on household pets, during his remaining twenty years.

In the course of his many and sometimes radical re-arrangements of his poems, Arnold revised his work very thoroughly. His revisions exemplify, among other things, his concern for 'literalness and sincerity', the qualities which he hoped in 1856 would always attract readers to his verse, though perhaps never in large numbers. Very rarely are his changes such as to lead a critical reader to hanker after the earlier, rejected versions. For this reason, the study of his poetry which follows is based upon the texts in that form in which he finally left them.

II

In a letter written in 1869, Arnold states that his poems 'represent, on the whole, the main movement of mind of the last quarter of a century'. There is some justifica-tion for this claim.

They represent, in the first place, the mid-nineteenth-century reaction against the extravagant fervours and expectations and idealisms of the Romantic generation. Like the novels of George Eliot, who was to find in later life that of all contemporary poetry Arnold's was that which kept growing upon her, they are much concerned with the conflict between these romantic aspirations and the rigorous, impartial, and inescapable tyranny of circumstance and natural law. Thus Arnold several times alludes to Byron, who

> taught us little; but our soul
> Had *felt* him like the thunder's roll.
> With shivering heart the strife we saw
> Of passion with eternal law;
> And yet with reverential awe
> We watch'd the fount of fiery life
> Which served for that Titanic strife.
>
> ('Memorial Verses.')

When he wrote this, Arnold clearly felt a spontaneous sympathy and admiration for Byron's revolt. But even then he knew that it was foredoomed to failure. Already, in 'Resignation', an early work which is manifestly assembled but in places equally manifestly felt, Arnold had preached the wisdom of submitting to 'time' and 'change', of learning 'to bear rather than rejoice'; and the protagonist of 'Empedocles on Etna', similarly, urges Pausanias to 'Nurse no extravagant hope' and to 'moderate desire' in the face of a universe which is utterly indifferent to him, which will in any case proceed in accordance with its own laws, and to which he will obviously be well-advised to adjust himself.

This picture of the universe as no longer 'peopled by Gods' ('Empedocles on Etna', II) was the achievement of the scientists and philosophers of what Carlyle called the age of victorious Analysis, the eighteenth century. From Blake onwards, the Romantics had rejected it. They could not destroy it, however. There was still for Clough the grim possibility that

> Earth goes by chemic forces; Heaven's
> A Mécanique Céleste;[1] ('The New Sinai.')

[1] The title of a work by Pierre Simon Laplace (1749–1827), the greatest theoretical astronomer since Newton.

and for Arnold the neutrality of the universe, the sense that

> the circumambient gloom
> But hides, if Gods, Gods careless of our doom,
> ('Mycerinus.')

heightened his already painful awareness of the inevitable
isolation of the individual human soul: 'We mortal
millions live *alone*' ('To Marguerite—Continued'). This
war between science and religion, reason and imagination, Bentham and Coleridge, is still being waged; it is
the fundamental conflict of this, as it was of the last,
century.

Arnold worked for a negotiated peace, a compromise.
He held that reason, in the shape of physical science and
German Biblical criticism, had already made belief in
the supernatural impossible for many people and that it
would quickly make it impossible for very many more.
Instead of joining Tennyson and Browning in denying
reason, Arnold characteristically accepted this growth of
scepticism as inevitable and asked how the moral and
other values traditionally associated with religion could
best be preserved in the circumstances. It is with this
question that he is preoccupied in 'Progress', which first
appeared in the 1852 volume, and in several of the
sonnets which he included in that of 1867.

His readiness to accept what he believed to be the
inevitable and to work within the limits imposed by it is
illustrated also by his dealings with 'the world'. Again
and again in his verse, Arnold describes the distracting and
bewildering and stupefying effect upon the individual of

> this strange disease of modern life,
> With its sick hurry, its divided aims,
> Its heads o'ertax'd, its palsied hearts.
> ('The Scholar-Gipsy.')

Seeking calm and self-possession, he withdraws from it
to the Alps, to the Grande Chartreuse, to the countryside
near Oxford which he had known in his youth, or
merely to Kensington Gardens. But he can never forget
that any but the briefest escape is impossible; he knows
that he must return almost at once. So he leaves the
Alps:

> I go, fate drives me; but I leave
> Half of my life with you.
>
> We, in some unknown Power's employ,
> Move on a rigorous line;
> Can neither, when we will, enjoy,
> Nor, when we will, resign.
> ('Stanzas in Memory of the Author of *Obermann*.')

The facetious comment which identifies the 'unknown
Power' with the Department of Education serves at least
to remind us that, unlike some of his immediate predecessors, Arnold was not protected by private income,
personal gift, sinecure, or legacy from the obligation of
working for a living in the ordinary Philistine sense of
the phrase. Because he knew it in his own life, Arnold
presents in his verse the dilemma of many who in the
modern world are compelled to live their lives in circumstances which fail to satisfy their natures, which
distract them indeed from learning what those natures
are, and which they must for their own well-being
periodically elude. If Arnold's landscapes are commonly
those of a week-ender—and the Georgian poets are
indeed his enfeebled successors—at least he also knew
and gave utterance to that unease which drives the week-
ender to the countryside.

It is, then, in several respects a representative consciousness that is apparent in Arnold's verse. His poems

describe simply and gravely his constant struggle to achieve stability, to make his romanticism submit to his realism, his unruly longings to his sense of things as they unalterably are. This is true whether his theme at the moment is his love for Marguerite or the decline of religious faith or 'this strange disease of modern life'. As a contemporary reviewer put it, 'Mr. Arnold's *sentiment*, his aspiration for life, is almost always in conflict with his critical perception of what life really is; . . . and hence he hits exactly many of the moods of an age which finds its desires for faith in strong contrast with what it deems the inadequate justification for those desires.'

But, while recognizing that Arnold does discuss in his verse many of the major interests which he shared with his more thoughtful and educated contemporaries, it still remains to ask whether he does so in such a way as to compel our imaginative participation—whether, in other words, he succeeds in making poetry out of them. My contention in the next section will be that he hardly ever does so.

III

In a letter to his sister Jane, written shortly after the publication of his 1849 volume, Arnold declares: 'At Oxford particularly many complain that the subjects treated do not interest them. But as I feel rather as a reformer in poetical matters, I am glad of this opposition. If I have health & opportunity to go on, I will shake the present methods until they go down, see if I don't. More and more I feel bent against the modern English habit (too much encouraged by Wordsworth) of using poetry as a channel for thinking aloud, instead of making

anything.' To Clough, similarly, he wrote at about the
same time that a certain friend 'urges me to speak more
from myself: which I less and less have the inclination
to do: or even the power'.

In keeping with these declarations, he speaks in his
first volume through the mouth of a Strayed Reveller, of
Mycerinus, of the Sick King in Bokhara; and in his
second he tries to assume more elaborate dramatic dis-
guises in 'Empedocles on Etna' and in 'Tristram and
Iseult'. But in none of these is his effort at 'making'
something, at 'grouping *objects*', entirely satisfactory.
His characters, in the situations in which he places them,
illustrate themes and conflicts of urgent importance to
him; but they lack the independent life without which
it is impossible for them effectively to impose themselves,
and thus to impose that which they are intended to
embody, upon our imaginations. Sometimes, either in
their own speeches or in his comments upon their
situations, they seem to be mere excuses for their creator
to indulge in that very 'thinking aloud' which he condemned; and elsewhere, more especially in the second
volume in such poems as 'The Buried Life', 'The Youth
of Nature', and 'The Youth of Man', thinking aloud is
offered without disguise.

> Murmur of living,
> Stir of existence,
> Soul of the world!
> Make, oh, make yourselves felt
> To the dying spirit of youth!
> Come, like the breath of the spring!
> Leave not a human soul
> To grow old in darkness and pain!
> Only the living can feel you,
> But leave us not while we live!

. . . While the locks are yet brown on thy head,
While the soul still looks through thine eyes,
While the heart still pours
The mantling blood to thy cheek,
Sink, O youth, in thy soul!
Yearn to the greatness of Nature;
Rally the good in the depths of thyself!

('The Youth of Man.')

These tired but faintly exclamatory ruminations are quite impotent as poetry.

Not that it is impossible to make poetry out of argumentation. In the finest passages of Pope's *Essay on Man* the thought is organized and phrased with such elegance that it attains the status of an object created for our contemplation, instead of that merely of something exuded by the poet. The impotence of Arnold's ruminations is due to the fact that in them very little is thus shaped and presented. He is guilty of 'thinking aloud'. In a selection of the language then used by poets, he gives us a lucid recital of a series of ideas, about our reception of which he evidently feels a trifle uneasy— hence his attempts to soften-up our resistance by a barrage of italics, interjections, and marks of exclamation. We are interested—nearly always, outside *Merope*, Arnold can count on that—but we are not surprised, disturbed, stimulated, and actively involved. 'Obermann Once More' is a good instance. Though it contains the interesting ideas which critics have found in it, they are stated less precisely, with less supporting detail, and with a less evident sense of their full range of implication than in Arnold's prose works. And the only thing added by the verse form is a distractingly glib, jog-trot rhythm:

Matthew Arnold in his late thirties

"*I say, the critic must keep out of the region of
immediate practice.*"

While we believed, on earth he went,
And open stood his grave.
Men call'd from chamber, church, and tent;
And Christ was by to save.

Arnold is more successful when, still consenting to
speak from himself, he associates his ruminations closely
with this or that particular landscape. To some extent he
does so in both of the poems from which I have just
quoted; but in each case the ruminations seem added to,
rather than indissolubly bound up with, the particular
landscape concerned. In his 'Rhapsody on a Windy
Night', Mr. T. S. Eliot is able to present a landscape and
the memories which it evokes in such a way as to suggest,
without ever describing, the observer's state of mind and
criticism of life. I am not blaming Arnold for not going
as far as this. But I think the contrast does show how
Arnold is afraid to rely on his symbolic landscape, how
he wishes to make everything fully explicit, and how, as
a result, he tends to add much rumination to a little
description and to call the total a poem.

This tendency is clearly visible in a small space in the
opening lines of 'Consolation':

> Mist clogs the sunshine.
> Smoky dwarf houses
> Hem me round everywhere;
> A vague dejection
> Weighs down my soul.

In the first three lines, Arnold presents what Mr. Eliot
might once have called an 'objective correlative' of his
state of mind. He presents it sketchily enough; but even
so it suffices to indicate his melancholy, his claustro-
phobia, his disgust at the meanness and ugliness of the life
around him. Instead of going on from there, however,

F

Arnold makes a fresh start with an explicit account
in general terms of his dejection; and in these terms he
can do no better than call it 'vague'. (A similar confession of failure occurs in 'The Buried Life': 'I feel a
nameless sadness o'er me roll.') It may be replied that
he called it vague because he really did find it impossible
to pin it down and trace its outlines. But a reference to
Edward Thomas should be enough to remind us of how
the indefinableness of an indefinable feeling can be conveyed by poetic means. Arnold merely asserts it.

'Consolation', written at least in part in 1849, is an
early poem. But the tendency can be traced even more
clearly in the opening paragraphs of 'A Summer Night':

> In the deserted, moon-blanch'd street,
> How lonely rings the echo of my feet!
> Those windows, which I gaze at, frown,
> Silent and white, unopening down,
> Repellent as the world;—but see,
> A break between the housetops shows
> The moon! and, lost behind her, fading dim
> Into the dewy dark obscurity
> Down at the far horizon's rim,
> Doth a whole tract of heaven disclose!
>
> And to my mind the thought
> Is on a sudden brought
> Of a past night, and a far different scene.
> Headlands stood out into the moonlit deep
> As clearly as at noon;
> The spring-tide's brimming flow
> Heaved dazzlingly between;
> Houses, with long white sweep,
> Girdled the glistening bay;
> Behind, through the soft air,
> The blue haze-cradled mountains spread away,
> That night was far more fair—

But the same restless pacings to and fro,
And the same vainly throbbing heart was there,
And the same bright, calm moon.

And the calm moonlight seems to say:
Hast thou then still the old unquiet breast,
Which neither deadens into rest,
Nor ever feels the fiery glow
That whirls the spirit from itself away,
But fluctuates to and fro,
Never by passion quite possess'd
And never quite benumb'd by the world's sway?—
And I, I know not if to pray
Still to be what I am, or yield and be
Like all the other men I see.

Like Mr. Eliot's, Arnold's street is held in a lunar syn-
thesis. Moonlight washes out the distracting multiplicity
of detail and colour visible by day; the simplified and
monochromatic world which it produces brings to mind
that relief from the multiple distractions and demands of
'modern life' for which Arnold craves. This craving is
implicit in the shift of his attention, essentially a movement of escape, from the repellent enclosing windows to
the free space of the 'whole tract of heaven'. A recol-
lected landscape follows; naturally, this, too, is moonlit.
It is not Dover; no 'blue haze-cradled mountains spread
away' from there. (Nor is it Thun, as sentimentalizers
of the Marguerite affair sometimes like to suggest; the
Swiss lakes are not tidal.) But the items of which it is
composed are very largely those out of which Arnold,
probably later, composed the landscape of his 'Dover
Beach'. The moonlight, the soft or sweet air, the cliffs
or headlands, the high tide, and even the metaphorical
girdle are evidently details with a symbolic value for the
poet who thus repeats himself. But the calm, stability,

and poise for which they stand are denied to him; and
from this thought the ruminations begin. Arnold tries
to work them in unobtrusively by having the moonlight
seem to address him, just as Mr. Eliot's street-lamps urge
him to remark various objects of interest in their vicinity.
But the moonlight is obviously Arnold talking to himself,
warning himself of the alternative dangers of the expense
of spirit in passion and the shrivelling of spirit in everyday
life in the world, that is, of the alternative dangers of
madness and slavery between which, in another poem,
his Iseult of Brittany has steered. Inevitably it all seems
too deliberate, too self-conscious; and the concluding
lines of the third paragraph are even Pharisaical.

In the later paragraphs, the toilers in the brazen prison
and the daring shipwrecked voyager are introduced to
illustrate these opposing dangers of slavery and madness.
But they are no more than illustrative. This is characteristic of Arnold. Broodingly, he states his thoughts;
he introduces apt if sometimes bookish examples; but
hardly ever does he create an aesthetically satisfying
object which will adequately embody his thoughts and
compel us, as we contemplate it, to relive them. After
an opening in which it seems possible that something of
the sort is going to emerge, 'A Summer Night' slips into
a series of lucid and despondent declarations which we
believe because we happen to know that Arnold was a
sincere man and not because they themselves force belief
upon us.

'A Summer Night' is by no means unique. Most of
'Resignation', both of the 'Obermann' elegies, the
'Stanzas from the Grande Chartreuse', 'Haworth Churchyard', 'Rugby Chapel', and 'Heine's Grave', all invite
description in similar terms. So does much of Empedocles' soliloquy on Etna.

Even the love poems exemplify something of the kind. When Arnold attempts a direct statement of his feelings in them the usual result is a rather frigid self-pity; the best of the 'Marguerite' poems are those in which his feelings are conveyed by a remembered dream ('A Dream') or a retold folk-tale ('The Forsaken Merman') or the imagined situation of islands, once part of a single continent, which are now separated by the sea ('To Marguerite—Continued'). Yet none even of these lyrics is perfect. The last of them, that beginning 'Yes! in the sea of life enisled', closes with an impressive stanza in which Arnold's characteristic conflict is epitomized in the curt finality of the antithesis 'kindled, cool'd'; and which leaves the reader sadly contemplating an 'unplumb'd, salt, estranging sea'. But the second stanza, with its 'moon', its 'balms of spring', and its 'nightingales' which 'divinely sing' their 'lovely notes', remains a tame and therefore ineffective catalogue of nineteenth-century poetic commonplaces.

'Dover Beach' is quite free from any trace of poeticality. It is a short poem, but in it Arnold relates the symbolic landscape which we have just glimpsed in 'A Summer Night' to ideas which are also prominent elsewhere in his work. The general decline of faith and Arnold's own resultant bewilderment and melancholy constitute the theme of the 'Stanzas from the Grande Chartreuse'; in 'The Buried Life', Arnold expresses the belief that in a successful love-relationship he may discover certain values which are not readily to be found in 'modern life'. Both of these ideas reappear in 'Dover Beach'. It would be in keeping with all that we know of the psychology of artists to suppose that a poem which is thus a crystallization of ideas given separate and less definitive expression elsewhere must be later in date than the poems in which they receive that separate and less definitive expression. 'Stanzas from the Grande Chartreuse', the later of the two poems thus linked with 'Dover Beach', refers to a visit which Arnold made to the monastery in September 1851, during his honeymoon; he was apparently working on the poem during 1852; and it was printed in a periodical in 1855, twelve years before its inclusion in *New Poems*. The implication seems to be that 'Dover Beach' must not be dated earlier than the middle years of this same decade. But no independent evidence is available to make this more than merely a critical intuition.

The 'moon-blanch'd' landscape described in the opening lines is composed of details which suggest the serenity, balance, and stability which Arnold desired for himself. This setting is evoked with considerable vividness.

> The sea is calm to-night.
> The tide is full, the moon lies fair
> Upon the straits;—on the French coast the light
> Gleams and is gone; the cliffs of England stand,
> Glimmering and vast, out in the tranquil bay.
> Come to the window, sweet is the night-air!
> Only, from the long line of spray
> Where the sea meets the moon-blanch'd land,
> Listen! you hear the grating roar
> Of pebbles which the waves draw back, and fling,
> At their return, up the high strand,
> Begin, and cease, and then again begin,
> With tremulous cadence slow, and bring
> The eternal note of sadness in.

We can point to the steady and weighty *rallentando* with which the first sentence completes its series of affirmations; to the contrasting tender appeal of the invitation which follows; and to the richness and fullness with which the sound and movement of the sea are rendered in the concluding eight lines. Examining these lines more closely, we can cite 'grating roar' as admirably conveying the two distinguishable but inseparable sounds made by waves breaking on shingle; we can acknowledge the almost physical stress given to the verbs 'draw back' and 'fling'; we can analyse up to a point the combination of syntactical and metrical means by which the ebbing and flowing motion of the waves is made actual; and we can admire the appropriateness of the Miltonic 'tremulous cadence slow' both as summarizing what has gone before and as permitting an easy and natural introduction of the 'eternal note of sadness'. But with all such comments we are in danger of substituting convenient but arbitrary rationalizations and simplifications for the rich complexity of our experience while reading the poem. The least inadequate criticism of any poem will always be that implicit in a reading of it aloud to an understanding hearer. Formal literary analysis can offer only a few crude indications of what one would be trying to do when giving such a reading.

The image which dominates this first paragraph of 'Dover Beach' forms part of the 'full view' described by Mr. W. H. Auden in his poem beginning, 'Look, stranger, on this island now'. Like Arnold, Mr. Auden appears in his poetry as a tortured intellectual concerned with working out his own salvation. His inferior work, and his admirers' preference for it, gave him during the nineteen-thirties a reputation as a political poet. This was misleading. At his best, Mr. Auden is a highly subjective poet; and like Arnold he tends to relate his mental states to symbolic landscapes. But, whereas Arnold's more successful landscapes seem to be apprehended by direct sensory experience, Mr. Auden's consist largely of items culled from atlases, newsreels, the daily press, and political, psychological, and other reading. In short, his characteristic landscapes appear to be known to the intelligence rather than to the senses. This is exemplified at an extreme in 'Spain 1937' and in the verse 'Commentary' which concludes the sonnet-sequence 'In Time of War'. Admittedly, Mr. Auden's early favourite landscape of industrial decay is sometimes rendered in potently sensuous terms; but this is unusual.

In the poem beginning, 'Look, stranger, on this island now', Mr. Auden seems again to have made the unusual effort to impose the landscape he is describing upon the very senses of his readers. The result is a good poem; but it would have been a better poem if the effort had been less obtrusively visible. The second stanza is all that concerns us now:

> Here at the small field's ending pause
> When the chalk wall falls to the foam and its tall ledges
> Oppose the pluck
> And knock of the tide,
> And the shingle scrambles after the suck-
> -ing surf
> And the gull lodges
> A moment on its sheer side.

The internal rhymes and successive emphatic beats in the second line, the aggressively tactile and kinaesthetic images introduced by 'pluck' and 'knock' in the third and fourth, and the onomatopoeic splitting of the word 'sucking' between the fifth and sixth are effective devices but too deliberate. It is precisely the effortlessness, the confident ease, of Arnold's description that is most remarkable when it is placed beside Mr. Auden's. Arnold is doing supremely well what comes naturally to him; Mr. Auden's description is, for him, a *tour de force*.

Having detected the 'eternal note of sadness', Arnold mentions a Sophoclean interpretation of it.

> Sophocles long ago
> Heard it on the Ægæan, and it brought
> Into his mind the turbid ebb and flow
> Of human misery; we
> Find also in the sound a thought,
> Hearing it by this distant northern sea.

The literary allusion serves not only to suggest that we have here to do with an archetypal image but also to introduce Arnold's own commentary.

This begins in a tone of straightforward exposition.

> The Sea of Faith
> Was once, too, at the full, and round earth's shore
> Lay like the folds of a bright girdle furl'd.

But instead of lapsing from this into rather flat rumination, which is what we have seen him do elsewhere, Arnold holds fast to the image of the sea. This has, so to speak, grown in his hands, so that it can now carry the whole weight of his feeling at the decline of religious faith. The symbol, so loaded, is presented in five haunting lines. The series of open vowels in the second of these, with the near-rhyme 'draw: roar', gives an eerie resonance which echoes down the remainder of the sentence with its 'falling' syntactical rhythm.

> But now I only hear
> Its melancholy, long, withdrawing roar,
> Retreating, to the breath
> Of the night-wind, down the vast edges drear
> And naked shingles of the world.

This is an early instance of the expressions of a horror of the utterly negative which occur from time to time in modern literature: in *A Passage to India* and *The Waste Land*, for example.

Critics acquainted with the extant manuscript of 'Dover Beach' sometimes complain that the last paragraph does not really belong with the remainder of the poem. In this draft, the last line is 'And naked shingles of the world. Ah love &c', which certainly suggests that the paragraph beginning 'Ah, love, let us be true' had already been written. But no amount of knowledge of its author's methods of composition can prove that a finished work is or is not a unified whole. With greater critical relevance, it may be argued that in this final paragraph Arnold has forgotten about the sea. But the sea has by this time served its purpose as a symbol; and that which it symbolized is still powerfully present in these last lines. Moreover, the darkness remains. Precisely because it is no longer possible to believe that the universe is in some degree adjusted to human needs, that it is informed by a divinity which sympathizes with men in their joys and sorrows and in their hopes and fears, the poet must seek in human love for those values which are undiscoverable elsewhere. Moreover—and this is the primary meaning of the last paragraph—the lovers must support each other if they are to live in the modern world without disaster.

> Ah, love, let us be true
> To one another! for the world, which seems
> To lie before us like a land of dreams,
> So various, so beautiful, so new,
> Hath really neither joy, nor love, nor light,
> Nor certitude, nor peace, nor help for pain;
> And we are here as on a darkling plain
> Swept with confused alarms of struggle and flight,
> Where ignorant armies clash by night.

As in the previous sentence, the main verb is introduced early; the result is what I have called a 'falling' syntactical rhythm, which contributes appreciably to the brooding melancholy of the whole paragraph. Metrically, this is the most regular section of the poem; after the initial short line, there are seven pentameters. The brief and therefore arresting last line carries the crucial phrase which discloses the full strangeness and horror of the concluding analogy. The

> darkling plain
> Swept with confused alarms of struggle and flight

is not remarkable; all the more powerful, therefore, is the harsh and surprising revelation, in the curtailed last line, of the nature of the battle: 'Where ignorant armies clash by night'. This image is Arnold's most impressive and most pregnant poetic utterance on 'modern life'.

'Dover Beach' is, I believe, his one great poem. As far as it is possible for a single short lyric to do so, it represents 'the main movement of mind of the last quarter of a century'; and it is the one work by Arnold which ought to appear in even the briefest anthology of great English poems. It may seem niggardly to limit such praise to a single work. But Arnold himself insists that excellence is rare; and a recognition of the uniqueness of 'Dover Beach' need not inhibit a warm admiration for other poems. Two more lyrics, 'Growing Old', possibly a retort to Browning's 'Rabbi ben Ezra' (1864), and 'Palladium', must certainly be included among these. The former, a series of brief, bare sentences, discloses with bitter sincerity 'the gifts reserved for age' ('Little Gidding'); the latter, in which Arnold handles Homeric names with something of a Yeatsian evocativeness, expresses his aspiration not to lose sight of spiritual values

even while in the thick of 'the battle in the plain'. Yet
even in these, and despite his feeling 'rather as a reformer
in poetical matters', his inability to free himself sufficiently from his age's preconceptions regarding what was
truly poetical is responsible for such phrases as 'Is it for
beauty to forego her wreath?' and

> Still doth the soul, from its lone fastness high,
> Upon our life a ruling effluence send.

A true reformer would have found it necessary to reform
the very language of poetry, as Gerard Manley Hopkins
was later to do.

Certain of Arnold's longer poems, too, call for particularly respectful attention—notably 'Empedocles on
Etna', the Oxford elegies ('The Scholar-Gipsy' and
'Thyrsis'), and 'Sohrab and Rustum'. An examination
of these should make it possible to define more closely
the conditions in which Arnold achieves his most complete poetic successes.

IV

At the head of a list of thirteen poems to be composed
during 1849, Arnold placed 'Empedocles—refusal of
limitation by the religious sentiment'. In the summer of
the same year, one of his friends wrote to Clough: 'I
saw the said Hero—Matt—the day I left London. He
goes in Autumn to the Tyrol with Slade. He was working at an "Empedocles"—which seemed to be not much
about the man who leapt in the crater—but his name &
outward circumstances are used for the drapery of his
own thoughts.' Arnold apparently went on working at
'Empedocles on Etna' until it was published as the title-
poem of his volume of 1852.

Naturally, he acquainted himself as closely as possible with the life and thought of the pre-Socratic philosopher-poet who was to be his hero. But Clough's informant was right in believing that such data provided a mere framework for the drama. Moreover, Arnold did not restrict himself to these as his only literary sources. Above the list of thirteen poems already mentioned, he wrote the words 'Chew Lucretius'. Lucretius was to some extent a disciple of Empedocles. Arnold had known his *De Natura Rerum*, a poem on the nature of the universe, since at least as early as 1845; and by 1849 he had certainly decided to make him the subject of a tragedy. He did much preparation for this play and probably never quite lost the hope of finishing it. That it nevertheless remained hardly begun even at his death was perhaps due to the fact that between 1849 and 1852 he gave expression in 'Empedocles on Etna' to much that would otherwise have gone into it. Thus, the three stanzas of Empedocles' hymn which begin

> Is it so small a thing
> To have enjoy'd the sun

were originally written for the Roman tragedy. But Arnold was an admirer also of Epictetus, of Marcus Aurelius, of Spinoza, and of Senancour. Accordingly his Empedocles, while voicing many of the ideas of the epicurean Lucretius, is fundamentally a stoic.

The complexity of this character as imagined by the poet is well brought out in Arnold's own prose memorandum of what he planned to depict.

> He is a philosopher.
> He has not the religious consolation of other men, facile because adapted to their weaknesses, or because shared by all around and changing the atmosphere they breathe.

He sees things as they are—the world as it is—God as he is: in their stern simplicity.

The sight is a severe and mind-tasking one: to know the mysteries which are communicated to others by fragments, in parables.

But he started towards it in hope: his first glimpses of it filled him with joy: he had friends who shared his hope & joy & communicated to him theirs: even now he does not deny that the sight is capable of affording rapture & the purest peace.

But his friends are dead: the world is all against him, & incredulous of the truth: his mind is overtasked by the effort to hold fast so great & severe a truth in solitude: the atmosphere he breathes not being modified by the presence of human life, is too rare for him. He perceives still the truth of the truth [*sic*], but cannot be transported and rapturously agitated by his grandeur: his spring and elasticity of mind are gone: he is clouded, oppressed, dispirited, without hope & energy.

Before he becomes the victim of depression & overtension of mind, to the utter deadness to joy, grandeur, spirit, and animated life, he desires to die; to be reunited with the universe, before by exaggerating his human side he has become utterly estranged from it.

Arnold's intention is further illuminated by a passage in his 'Preface' of 1853 in which he explains why he has suppressed 'Empedocles on Etna'.

I have done so, not because the subject of it was a Sicilian Greek born between two and three thousand years ago, although many persons would think this a sufficient reason. Neither have I done so because I had, in my own opinion, failed in the delineation which I intended to effect. I intended to delineate the feelings of one of the last of the Greek religious philosophers, one of the family of Orpheus and Musaeus, having survived his fellows, living on into a time when the habits of Greek thought and feeling had begun fast to change, character to dwindle, the influence of the Sophists to prevail. Into the feelings of a man so situated there entered much that we are accustomed to consider as exclusively modern; how much, the fragments of Empedocles himself which remain to us are sufficient at least to indicate. What those who are familiar only with the great monuments of early Greek genius suppose to be its exclusive characteristics, have disappeared; the calm, the cheerfulness, the disinterested objectivity have disappeared: the dialogue of the mind with itself has commenced; modern problems have presented themselves; we hear already the doubts, we witness the discouragement, of Hamlet and of Faust.

The representation of such a man's feelings must be interesting, if consistently drawn. We all naturally take pleasure, says Aristotle, in any imitation or representation whatever . . . ; but, if the representation be a poetical one, more than this is demanded. It is demanded, not only that it shall interest, but also that it shall inspirit and rejoice the reader: that it shall convey a charm, and infuse delight. . . .

What then are the situations, from the representation of which, though accurate, no poetical enjoyment can be derived? They are those in which the suffering finds no vent in action; in which a continuous state of mental distress is prolonged, unrelieved by incident, hope, or resistance; in which there is everything to be endured, nothing to be done. In such situations there is inevitably something morbid, in the description of them something monotonous. When they occur in actual life, they are painful, not tragic; the representation of them in poetry is painful also.

To this class of situations, poetically faulty as it appears to me, that of Empedocles, as I have endeavoured to represent him, belongs; and I have therefore excluded the Poem from the present collection.

During the fourteen years following this declaration, Arnold allowed only the five songs of Callicles and a short passage from Empedocles' soliloquy to be reprinted.

Then, in 1867, he reissued the whole work 'at the request of a man of genius, whom it had the honour and the good fortune to interest,—Mr. Robert Browning'.

'Empedocles on Etna' is virtually a monodrama. Apart from the protagonist, only two characters appear: Pausanias, a physician, a 'good, learned, friendly, quiet man', the confidant of Empedocles, the Horatio or Wagner to his Hamlet or Faust; and Callicles, a young harp-player, well loved by Empedocles and strangely drawn to him in his turn. The unhappy Empedocles is seeking solitude on Etna. Pausanias, accompanying him for part of the ascent, hopes to learn from him the secret of a miracle which he is said to have performed. Callicles, curious and anxious at their departure from the city, has followed them surreptitiously.

The poem opens with Callicles, who has outstripped the others, waiting shortly after dawn for them to come upon him as they continue their ascent. His opening soliloquy describes, in phrases sometimes reminiscent of Keats, the kind of setting which is common to both scenes of Act I:

> the sun
> Is shining on the brilliant mountain-crests,
> And on the highest pines; but farther down,
> Here in the valley, is in shade; the sward
> Is dark, and on the stream the mist still hangs;
> One sees one's footprints crush'd in the wet grass,
> One's breath curls in the air; and on these pines
> That climb from the stream's edge, the long grey tufts,
> Which the goats love, are jewell'd thick with dew.

Coolness and freshness are qualities which Arnold repeatedly opposes to those belonging to 'the broiling city'.

Pausanias discovers the young harp-player before Empedocles' arrival. He insists that Callicles keep out of the

Matthew Arnold. -

1883.

1.

Bradshaw

Sohrab and Rustum.   (Print Rustum throughout)

An Episode.

And the first grey of morning fill'd the east,
And the fog rose out of the Oxus stream.
But all the Tartar camp along the stream
Was hush'd, and still the men were plung'd in sleep:
Sohrab alone, he slept not: all night long
He had lain wakeful, tossing on his bed;
But when the grey dawn stole into his tent,
He rose, and clad himself, and girt his sword,
And took his horseman's cloak, and left his tent,
And went abroad into the cold wet fog,
Through the dim camp to Peran-Wisa's tent.

Through the black Tartar tents he pass'd, which stood
Clustering like beehives on the low flat strand
Of Oxus, where the summer floods o'erflow
When the sun melts the snows in high Pamere:
Through the black tents he pass'd, o'er that low strand,
And to a hillock came; a little back
From the stream's brink, the spot where first a boat
Crossing the stream in summer, scrapes the leafy.
The men of former times had crown'd the top
With a clay fort: but that was fall'n; and now
The Tartars built there Peran-Wisa's tent,

The manuscript of the opening lines of Sohrab
and Rustum

philosopher's sight—'One of his moods is on him that
thou know'st'—but allows him to try the effect of his
music from a distance upon the 'lonely man in triple
gloom'. Pausanias is inclined to ascribe Empedocles' un-
happiness to external causes such as his banishment from
his own city and the alleged hostility of the sophists. But
Callicles asserts that Empedocles' misery is due to factors
within himself:

> 'Tis not the times, 'tis not the sophists vex him;
> There is some root of suffering in himself,
> Some secret and unfollow'd vein of woe,
> Which makes the time look black and sad to him.

This is confirmed by Empedocles' soliloquy, which
occupies almost the whole of Act II and concludes with
his suicide.

In 1867 Arnold denied that he had used Empedocles
to express his own views. He pointed out that 'if
Empedocles throws himself into Etna his creed can
hardly be meant to be one to live by'. Nevertheless, it
is impossible to disbelieve entirely the friend who, in
1849, said that Arnold was using Empedocles' name and
outward circumstances 'for the drapery of his own
thoughts'. The truth seems to be that while Arnold
could quite honestly dissociate himself in 1867 from
many of his protagonist's views, Empedocles' soliloquy
had, in 1852, expressed for his creator a possible outcome
of tendencies in himself of which he was only too well
aware. When, moreover, we turn back from the soliloquy to the long hymn which occupies almost the whole
of the previous scene, I. ii, we find Empedocles expressing views which are indistinguishable from those which
Arnold either advanced elsewhere or may very reasonably
be supposed to have entertained at the time of writing.

G

In this hymn Empedocles, accompanying himself for the last time on his harp, advises Pausanias on how so feeble a creature as man may best approach happiness in a universe which is totally indifferent to his welfare. In its metrical form the hymn is reminiscent of Shelley's ode 'To a Skylark'. The chief difference is that Arnold, wishing to unfold a consecutive argument, uses the rhyming syllables of the alexandrines to link the stanzas in pairs. His feeling is so far from the Shelleyan ecstasy that the hymn is quite prosaic. But its argument is interesting.

Empedocles begins by comparing man's fragmentary and disjointed vision of life with the series of images caught in a hanging mirror spinning in, and driving before, the winds. 'Is fate indeed so strong,' he asks, 'man's strength indeed so poor?' But his question is merely rhetorical. In what follows, he tacitly assumes an affirmative answer and substitutes for the metaphysical question an ethical one: How can man make the best of his precarious situation?

His advice to unhappy mankind is that of the stoics: 'Sink in thyself! there ask what ails thee, at that shrine!' Man is discontented, he struggles, raves, and is ill at ease, because he cherishes the delusive belief that the world exists for his benefit and that he has a natural right to happiness. (In making Empedocles repudiate the doctrine of natural rights, Arnold is following his father and Coleridge and Burke.) It is not wrong for man to seek happiness; but he is mistaken in supposing that he is entitled to it:

> Man errs not that he deems
> His welfare his true aim,
> He errs because he dreams
> The world does but exist that welfare to bestow.

The world goes on in its own, and not in our, way:

> In vain our pent wills fret,
> And would the world subdue.
> Limits we did not set
> Condition all we do;
> Born into life we are, and life must be our mould.

A wise man would seek happiness only within the limits imposed by circumstances. But most of us are unwise; and our immoderate expectations bring us to grief.

This ought to dispel our self-pleasing delusions. It does not, however. For we invent hostile gods upon whom to blame our misfortunes, 'With God and Fate to rail at, suffering easily.' Moreover, we invent kind gods who in some future state will satisfy those of our desires which are thwarted here and now. Empedocles is harshly scornful of such shifts:

> Fools! That so often here
> Happiness mock'd our prayer,
> I think, might make us fear
> A like event elsewhere;
> Make us, not fly to dreams, but moderate desire.

These last two words, 'moderate desire', epitomize his advice to his credulous friend.

An attempt to present this doctrine in as cheerful a light as possible concludes the hymn:

> Is it so small a thing
> To have enjoy'd the sun,
> To have lived light in the spring,
> To have loved, to have thought, to have done;
> To have advanced true friends, and beat down baffling
>   foes—

That we must feign a bliss
Of doubtful future date,
And, while we dream on this,
Lose all our present state,
And relegate to worlds yet distant our repose?

. . . But thou, because thou hear'st
Men scoff at Heaven and Fate,
Because the Gods thou fear'st
Fail to make blest thy state,
Tremblest, and wilt not dare to trust the joys there
      are!

I say: Fear not! Life still
Leaves human effort scope.
But, since life teems with ill,
Nurse no extravagant hope;
Because thou must not dream, thou need'st not then
      despair!

There is nothing blissful or rapturous about the life which Empedocles recommends to Pausanias. But to a poet as deeply infected by the sceptical spirit of his age as Arnold it must have seemed to offer the nearest approach to happiness compatible with the human situation.

It cannot, however, satisfy Empedocles himself. Dismissing Pausanias, he climbs beyond the last of 'all the woody, high, well-water'd dells' which have provided settings for the two scenes of the relatively genial Act I; and at the beginning of Act II he is, in his own words,

Alone!—
On this charr'd, blacken'd, melancholy waste,
Crown'd by the awful peak, Etna's great mouth,
Round which the sullen vapour rolls—alone!

This setting is entirely appropriate for a soliloquy expounding and exemplifying his deterioration into

> Nothing but a devouring flame of thought—
> But a naked, eternally restless mind!

Empedocles cannot deny that he has been a 'slave of thought'; and his bondage has resulted in the drying-up of his spirit's 'self-sufficing fount of joy'. His sickness resembles that which Arnold knew and feared in himself when he adopted a pose of dandyism in order to protect himself against the Rugby and Oxford depth-hunters of his acquaintance. But in Empedocles the disease is mortal. His suicide is a bold symbol of the ultimate destruction of the human person by the 'devouring flame' of arid self-consciousness and restless speculation.

In the blank verse and occasional free verse of his soliloquy, he expresses himself with an ease and a naturalness which he rarely achieves in the short lines, constricting because demanding so rapid a succession of rhyming syllables, of his hymn. Much of the speech, nevertheless, remains uncreatively ruminative. Its content, very largely that of Arnold's prose memorandum already quoted, is interesting. Empedocles' complaint that in the uncongenial age into which he has survived

> Great qualities are trodden down,
> And littleness united
> Is become invincible

reminds us that his creator belonged to a generation keenly aware of the dangers which might arise from the growth of democracy; and his confession of dismay at the thought of the neutrality of a universe no longer 'peopled by Gods', a confession which Pausanias' presence has presumably inhibited until now, echoes what

Arnold writes elsewhere. But it is only towards the end of the soliloquy that Empedocles' utterance gains urgency and life.

He has discarded the insignia both of his former 'un-loved preëminence' among men and of the poetic office which kept him apart from them in solitude. Having come to ascribe to a failure of vitality in himself his feeling that the universe has lost its divinity, he longs for an end to be put to the restless thought and self-questioning which have crippled him. He is content that his physical being should revert to the elements from which it was formed.

> But mind, but thought—
> If these have been the master part of us—
> Where will *they* find their parent element?
> What will receive *them*, who will call *them* home?
> But we shall still be in them, and they in us,
> And we shall be the strangers of the world,
> And they will be our lords, as they are now;
> And keep us prisoners of our consciousness,
> And never let us clasp and feel the All
> But through their forms, and modes, and stifling veils.
> And we shall be unsatisfied as now;
> And we shall feel the agony of thirst,
> The ineffable longing for the life of life
> Baffled for ever; and still thought and mind
> Will hurry us with them on their homeless march,
> Over the unallied unopening earth,
> Over the unrecognising sea; while air
> Will blow us fiercely back to sea and earth,
> And fire repel us from its living waves.
> And then we shall unwillingly return
> Back to this meadow of calamity,
> This uncongenial place, this human life;
> And in our individual human state

Go through the sad probation all again,
To see if we will poise our life at last,
To see if we will now at last be true
To our own only true, deep-buried selves,
Being one with which we are one with the whole world;
Or whether we will once more fall away
Into some bondage of the flesh or mind,
Some slough of sense, or some fantastic maze
Forged by the imperious lonely thinking-power.
And each succeeding age in which we are born
Will have more peril for us than the last;
Will goad our senses with a sharper spur,
Will fret our minds to an intenser play,
Will make ourselves harder to be discern'd.
And we shall struggle awhile, gasp and rebel—
And we shall fly for refuge to past times,
Their soul of unworn youth, their breath of greatness;
And the reality will pluck us back,
Knead us in its hot hand, and change our nature
And we shall feel our powers of effort flag,
And rally them for one last fight—and fail;
And we shall sink in the impossible strife,
And be astray for ever.

This is Arnold's finest passage of blank verse; and it is a genuinely dramatic speech. The repetitive sequences of harassed and despairing utterances, each one receiving very much the same degree of emphasis as its neighbours, convey insidiously the bewilderment of men driven hither and thither by 'thought and mind'; and the larger rhythm which unites the sequences carries us on, unrestingly and dizzily, to the desolate silence which follows the words 'And be astray for ever'.

While this speech describes and exemplifies what Arnold feared, and while Empedocles' hymn defines the utmost for which Arnold thought it prudent to hope, the five songs of Callicles express collectively a less realistic impulse. They are a product of Arnold's recurrent wistful yearning to escape from the 'darkling plain' to some place—early Greece, the countryside around Oxford, or the Alps—which is less inimical to the achievement of a joyful serenity. It was evidently his intention that they should exhibit the characteristics which, in his 'Preface' of 1853, he attributed to the early Greek genius, namely, calm, cheerfulness, and disinterested objectivity; and that Callicles, as the youthful exponent of these values, should stand in contrast with Empedocles, who represents the doubts and discouragement, 'the dialogue of the mind with itself', which are endemic on the 'darkling plain'. Callicles' qualities were to be those which Arnold, as a good Goethean, wished to realize in his poetry and for the sake of which he tried as a young man to hold himself a little aloof from his more Empedoclean friends. But in reading Callicles' songs we are less aware of a beautiful objectivity than of Arnold's plaintive longing to be 'Far, far from here', to be, perhaps,

> where Helicon breaks down
> In cliff to the sea.

These songs have great charm; but they have not the actuality and point of the lines I have quoted from Empedocles' soliloquy.

Nevertheless, they provide welcome relief from the sombre monologues of the introspective sage. It seems to have been Arnold's intention that each of them should have also a special relevance to the context in which it is placed. The first of them relates how Chiron, the aged centaur, imparted to the young Achilles an intimate understanding of natural things. His doctrine of nature contrasts with the harsher one preached by Empedocles in the hymn which immediately follows. After the hymn, Callicles sings of the placid and dumb contentment of Cadmus and Harmonia, metamorphosed in their old age and removed far from the scenes of 'their first sad life'. Again, a contrast seems to be implied. Empedocles,

> whose youth fell on a different world
> From that on which his exiled age is thrown,

can achieve no such peace of mind as theirs. It is interesting to note that 'Cadmus and Harmonia' remained one of Arnold's favourites among his poems throughout his life.

Early in Act II, Callicles sings of Typho, the rebellious Titan whom Zeus subdued and buried beneath Etna. He ends with a picture of Zeus himself sitting with his fellow-Olympians. But Empedocles' sympathy goes out to Typho; he sees his fate as symbolizing the defeat everywhere of the 'brave, impetuous heart' by 'the subtle, contriving head'; and in his bitterness he strips himself of the insignia of his power. When Callicles interrupts him again with the story of Apollo's triumph over Marsyas, Empedocles' self-pity once more leads him to side with the victim, and the song celebrating the triumph of poetry becomes the immediate occasion of his forswearing poetry. Callicles' voice is not heard again until after Empedocles' death. He then concludes the poem with a joyful hymn to Apollo which switches the reader's attention from Etna to Helicon and Olympus.

As a dramatic poem, 'Empedocles on Etna' is a failure. None of its three personages seems to speak or to act from an independent centre of vitality. Even if, changing our ground, we judge it as a body of subjective poetry, the verdict cannot be very much more favourable. Admittedly, the songs of Callicles have an authentic if conventionally poetical charm. But only once, in the passage quoted from the end of Empedocles' soliloquy, does the verse approach greatness. At the same time, both the general plan of the work and in many places the particular ideas which the characters express are genuinely interesting. It is, in fact, 'with more interest than rapture', as G. M. Hopkins wrote in 1873, that we read both this and most of Arnold's other poems.

Owing to its imperfections as a dramatic creation, the work is in practice less painful than Arnold feared when he suppressed it in 1853. It is worth noting, however, that the optimistic George Meredith was moved to a high-spirited protest:

> And this great Doctor, can it be,
> He left no saner recipe
> For men at issue with despair?
> Admiring, even his poet owns,
> While noting his fine lyric tones,
> The last of him was heels in air! ('Empedocles.')

V

It was in Joseph Glanvill's *The Vanity of Dogmatizing* (1661) that Arnold found the story of an Oxford scholar who left his studies 'to joyn himself to a company of *Vagabond Gypsies*' and who hoped in time to learn from them the secret of their hypnotic powers. Arnold acquired his copy of this work in 1844 but left it unread at least until the autumn of the following year. Between then and 1849 he decided to write a poem about the scholar-gipsy. The twelfth item in his list, already mentioned, of thirteen poems to be composed during 1849 is 'The first mesmerist'. Another list, drawn up about two years later, names this 'the wandering Mesmerist'.

The difference between the two titles is indicative of the direction in which the poem was developing. When it was published in 1853 there was little in it about the then fashionable science of mesmerism. But its hero was nothing if not a wanderer.

Arnold imagines him as still roaming through the countryside around Oxford, 'Seen by rare glimpses, pensive and tongue-tied'. In the stanzas describing how both rustics and Oxford men have had fleeting glimpses of him, these three characteristics are insisted upon and exemplified. He flies from the noisy company of 'smock-frock'd boors' and 'Oxford riders blithe'; he loves 'retired ground'; he haunts 'shy retreats' and 'shy fields and distant Wychwood bowers'; and at night he seeks his 'straw in some sequester'd grange'. Crossing a stream by punt, he leans backwards 'in a pensive dream'; house-wives and children have known him 'hanging on a gate' —like the poet in 'Resignation'—and giving up the entire day to contemplation of the life around him; others have been able to note his gipsy attire, 'hat of antique shape, and cloak of grey', and, more important, his 'soft abstracted air'. He speaks to nobody.

He is a lonely figure. He hopes to learn and to make known the gipsies' 'arts to rule . . . men's brains'; but, he says, 'it needs heaven-sent moments for this skill'. So we see him not so much consorting with the gipsies as waiting in solitude 'for the spark from heaven to fall'. Evidently more is in question than merely the technique of mesmerism. So much more that definition is impossible. All we can say is that some mysterious wisdom is the true object of his incessant wandering.

While his object can be described only in such general terms as these, the settings in which he is glimpsed are often most sharply and most vividly rendered. In

conjunction with the setting in which the poet himself
first appears, reading Glanvill's book and exhorting the
'shepherd' to renew the quest of the scholar, they constitute one of the finest of Arnold's symbolic landscapes,
perfectly adapted to solitary, calm, and refreshing medita-
tion. We see the scholar, for example,

> Crossing the stripling Thames at Bab-lock-hithe,
>   Trailing in the cool stream thy fingers wet,
>   As the punt's rope chops round.

The word 'stripling' has, over and above its immediate
aptness, a wider relevancy in a poem so much concerned
with its author's own youth. For 'The Scholar-Gipsy'
embodies and expresses Arnold's intimate knowledge of
and love for the countryside near Oxford which he had
explored years earlier with Clough and Walrond and his
own brother Tom. In a letter addressed to Tom in
1857 he writes that the poem 'was meant to fix the
remembrance of those delightful wanderings of ours . . .
before they were quite effaced'. This intention is clearly
evident in such a stanza as the following:

> And, above Godstow Bridge, when hay-time's here
>   In June, and many a scythe in sunshine flames,
>   Men who through those wide fields of breezy grass
>   Where black-wing'd swallows haunt the glittering
>   Thames,
>   To bathe in the abandon'd lasher pass,
>   Have often pass'd thee near
>   Sitting upon the river bank o'ergrown;
>   Mark'd thine outlandish garb, thy figure spare,
>   Thy dark vague eyes, and soft abstracted air—
>   But, when they came from bathing, thou wast gone!

The opening lines of this stanza, with their sharp
outlining of the 'black-wing'd swallows' against the

dazzling landscape, are as Keatsian as those quoted earlier from Callicles. In its metrical structure, too, it is reminiscent of the stanzas of Keats' great odes. This influence pervades 'The Scholar-Gipsy' but is particularly marked in the earlier, descriptive part with which we have so far been exclusively concerned. The last stanza of this part, in which Arnold tells himself that he is merely dreaming when he pictures the scholar as still roaming the countryside, provides another clear example :

> thou from earth art gone
> Long since, and in some quiet churchyard laid—
> Some country-nook, where o'er thy unknown grave
> Tall grasses and white flowering nettles wave,
> Under a dark, red-fruited yew-tree's shade.

The transition to the second part of the work is effected by a turn which again recalls Keats. Having assured himself that the scholar is dead, the poet immediately rises in protest against the assertion. 'No, no,' he declares, 'thou hast not felt the lapse of hours!' and in the next stanza he goes on virtually to paraphrase the argument of the sixth and seventh stanzas of the 'Ode to a Nightingale' : 76142

> The generations of thy peers are fled,
> And we ourselves shall go;
> But thou possessest an immortal lot.

This immortality of the scholar is due to his having had '*one* aim, *one* business, *one* desire'. He left the world early,

> with powers
> Fresh, undiverted to the world without,
> Firm to their mark, not spent on other things;
> Free from the sick fatigue, the languid doubt,
> Which much to have tried, in much been baffled, brings.
> O life unlike to ours!

He waits for the spark from heaven. So do we, 'Light
half-believers of our casual creeds', but without his hope.
Sadly the poet exhorts him,

> O born in days when wits were fresh and clear,
>   And life ran gaily as the sparkling Thames;
>   Before this strange disease of modern life,
>   With its sick hurry, its divided aims,
>   Its heads o'ertax'd, its palsied hearts, was rife—
>   Fly hence, our contact fear!
>   Still fly, plunge deeper in the bowering wood!
>   Averse, as Dido did with gesture stern
>   From her false friend's approach in Hades turn,
>   Wave us away, and keep thy solitude!
>
> Still nursing the unconquerable hope,
>   Still clutching the inviolable shade,
>   With a free, onward impulse brushing through,
>   By night, the silver'd branches of the glade—
>   Far on the forest-skirts, where none pursue,
>   On some mild pastoral slope
>   Emerge, and resting on the moonlit pales
>   Freshen thy flowers as in former years
>   With dew, or listen with enchanted ears,
>   From the dark dingles, to the nightingales!
>
> But fly our paths, our feverish contact fly!
>   For strong the infection of our mental strife,
>   Which, though it gives no bliss, yet spoils for rest;
>   And we should win thee from thy own fair life,
>   Like us distracted, and like us unblest.
>   Soon, soon thy cheer would die,
>   Thy hopes grow timorous, and unfix'd thy powers,
>   And thy clear aims be cross and shifting made;
>   And then thy glad perennial youth would fade,
>   Fade, and grow old at last, and die like ours.

This is poetry of great charm. But it is poetry which belongs too completely to the world of poetry. It lacks the reality and urgency of the best of Arnold's Empedoclean verse. The first and third stanzas state clearly enough the predicament of those who dwell on the 'darkling plain'. But their predicament is not brought home to us as by the concluding image of 'Dover Beach' or the compelling rhythm of the last long paragraph of Empedocles' soliloquy. Instead, the statement is gracefully couched in conventionally poetical terms.

As for the second stanza, which movingly recalls the symbolic landscape presented earlier in the poem, what are we to make of 'the unconquerable hope', or, as it is named elsewhere, the 'mark', the '*one* aim, *one* business, *one* desire', of the scholar? It is difficult to believe that Arnold had any very exact conception of what he meant by these terms. What does emerge is that the possession of '*one* aim, *one* business, *one* desire' gives immortality to the scholar by protecting him against the 'strange disease' not only of 'modern life' but also of human life as such:

> For what wears out the life of mortal men?
>   'Tis that from change to change their being rolls;
> 'Tis that repeated shocks, again, again,
>   Exhaust the energy of strongest souls
>   And numb the elastic powers.

In fact, the scholar personifies an impulse of pure evasion. If the predicament from which Arnold wishes to escape is given little or no poetic substance, the secret for which he craves is almost as vague as the objective proposed in Longfellow's 'Excelsior'. What the poem really offers is a very delightful pastoral week-end. Arnold's indebtedness in it to the Keats who presided over the nineteenth-century poetry of the dream-world ought not to surprise us.

The poem ends with a coda which transports us to the early Greek world of which Callicles elsewhere is a belated representative. In this, a 'grave Tyrian trader' discovers that a 'merry Grecian coaster',

> Freighted with amber grapes, and Chian wine,
> Green, bursting figs, and tunnies steep'd in brine,

has put in at one of the Ægæan isles which he had been accustomed to regard as his own territory. He recognizes in these 'intruders on his ancient home' the 'young lighthearted masters of the waves'. He immediately turns from them, sails 'indignantly' to the western Mediterranean and out into the Atlantic, and begins to trade with those 'Shy traffickers, the dark Iberians', undoing 'his corded bales' upon the beach for this purpose.

In itself, this is a pleasing episode. But the thread which attaches it to the main body of the poem is very tenuous. Arnold introduces the Tyrian trader ostensibly in order to illustrate his advice to the scholar to 'fly our greetings, fly our speech and smiles!' But surely the scholar, with his 'unclouded joy' and his 'glad perennial youth' has more in common with the 'young lighthearted masters of the waves' than with the 'grave Tyrian' who flies 'indignantly' from them? Certainly the 'merry' Greeks could hardly offer a more complete contrast than they do with the palsied denizens of the 'darkling plain' with whom they are apparently equated. With rather more appropriateness, 'the dark Iberians' may be taken to correspond with the gipsies to whom the scholar has turned.

Several commentators have tried to demonstrate the relevance of this simile, usually by stressing the aloofness which the Tyrian shares with the scholar and by equating the Greeks with the 'smock-frock'd boors' and 'Oxford riders blithe' whom the scholar shuns. But there is nothing in the poetry to limit and direct our responses in this fashion. The interpretation is merely ingenious.

This is not the only poem of Arnold's to end with such a coda. On the contrary, the device was a favourite with him. It occurs, for example, in 'Tristram and Iseult', 'Sohrab and Rustum', and 'Stanzas from the Grande Chartreuse'. His intention was evidently to round off each of these longer poems with a digression which would give some relief to the reader by taking his mind off the melancholy main theme of the work and which would at the same time redirect his attention to what was essential in that main theme by presenting a symbolic equivalent of it. Perhaps the final simile of 'The Scholar-Gipsy' performs the first of these functions; it can hardly be said to perform the second.

Arnold was not altogether satisfied with the poem. In the year of its publication, he wrote to Clough: 'I am glad you like the Gipsy Scholar—but what does it *do* for you? Homer *animates*—Shakespeare *animates*—in its poor way I think Sohrab and Rustum *animates*—the Gipsy Scholar at best awakens a pleasing melancholy. But this is not what we want.

> The complaining millions of men
> Darken in labour and pain—[1]

what they want is something to *animate* and *ennoble* them —not merely to add zest to their melancholy or grace to their dreams.' Others are unlikely to share Arnold's uneasiness at the mere melancholy of the poem. After all, a much more urgent, even desperate, pessimism characterizes his very finest work. But when he says that the poem 'at best awakens a pleasing melancholy', that

---

[1] Quoted from 'The Youth of Nature'.

H

it merely 'adds zest' to men's melancholy or 'grace to
their dreams', he implies a criticism of it which is likely
to gain much wider acceptance: he implies that there is
something relaxing or enervating about it. This implication is so completely in line with the criticism of the
poem which I have already made that I see no point in
elaborating it now. All I wish to add is the suggestion
that 'The Scholar-Gipsy' is the finest of the poems which
may be taken to express the impulse which created
Callicles.

The 'shepherd' addressed at the beginning of the poem
was probably Clough; so it is not surprising that Arnold's
elegy on him should have taken the form of a sequel to
'The Scholar-Gipsy'. 'Thyrsis' is set in the same sur-
roundings and written in the same metrical form; and
the wandering scholar appears three times in it.

'I shall some day', wrote Arnold within a week of
receiving the news of Clough's death, 'in some way or
other relieve myself of what I think about him.' He
declined an invitation to contribute an obituary notice to
a newspaper. But before the end of the same month,
November 1861, he spoke warmly of his friend in the
last of his Oxford lectures on translating Homer, praising
him for the integrity of his literary life. Early in 1862
he was thinking of visiting the places near Oxford which
they had known as young men; and by the spring of
1863 he had formed the plan of writing 'a new poem
about the Cumner hillside, and Clough in connexion with
it'. He seems not to have started this poem until 1864.

'Thyrsis' was first published in a periodical in 1866.
Arnold said that the 'diction of the poem was modelled
on that of Theocritus, whom I have been much reading
during the two years this poem has been forming itself'
and that he 'meant the diction to be so artless as to be

almost heedless'. In another letter he admitted that there
was much in Clough, 'the whole *prophet* side, in fact',
which could not be dealt with in the poem as he had
conceived it and that 'one has the feeling, if one reads
the poem as a memorial poem, that not enough is said
about Clough in it. . . . Still Clough *had* this idyllic
side, too; to deal with this suited my desire to deal
again with that Cumner country: anyway, only so could
I treat the matter this time.'

Clough receives much more attention in 'Thyrsis'
than does either Edward King in 'Lycidas' or Keats in
'Adonais'. Nor does Arnold entirely neglect the *'prophet
side'* of him. Writing in the Theocritan pastoral convention, he explains Clough's departure from Oxford by
saying that the shepherd Thyrsis could not contentedly
accept the bucolic life he loved because

> Some life of men unblest
> He knew, which made him droop, and fill'd his head.
> He went; his piping took a troubled sound
> Of storms that rage outside our happy ground;
> He could not wait their passing, he is dead.

Towards the end of the poem he repeats this account of
Clough's career:

> the music of thy rustic flute
> Kept not for long its happy, country tone;
> Lost it too soon, and learnt a stormy note
> Of men contention-tost, of men who groan,
> Which task'd thy pipe too sore, and tired thy throat—
> It fail'd, and thou wast mute!

Later in this same stanza, the phrase 'men of care' may
well refer to the society which Clough entered as Principal
of University Hall—'Doubting Castle', in Arnold's eyes—
and which he soon left to resume his 'wandering way'.

Nevertheless, the poem is not primarily a portrait of Clough. It is an expression of Arnold's own persistent longing to relive those early days when he and Clough had rambled in the Cumnor hills together.

> I know these slopes; who knows them if not I?—
>   But many a dingle on the loved hill-side,
>   With thorns once studded, old, white-blossom'd trees,
>   Where thick the cowslips grew, and far descried
>   High tower'd the spikes of purple orchises,
>   Hath since our day put by
>   The coronals of that forgotten time;
>   Down each green bank hath gone the ploughboy's team,
>   And only in the hidden brookside gleam
>   Primroses, orphans of the flowery prime.
>
> Where is the girl, who by the boatman's door,
>   Above the locks, above the boating throng,
>   Unmoor'd our skiff when through the Wytham flats,
>   Red loosestrife and blond meadow-sweet among
>   And darting swallows and light water-gnats,
>   We track'd the shy Thames shore?
>   Where are the mowers, who, as the tiny swell
>   Of our boat passing heaved the river-grass,
>   Stood with suspended scythe to see us pass?—
>   They are all gone, and thou art gone as well!

Arnold confessed to a special fondness for these two stanzas; 'but', he added, 'that is because they bring certain places and moments before me.'

It is worth noting that the 'darting swallows' and the epithet 'shy', here applied to the 'Thames shore', are among the many details which connect the symbolic landscape of this poem with that of 'The Scholar-Gipsy'. But an important feature is added to it in 'Thyrsis'. This is the 'signal-elm' which crowns the 'hill behind whose ridge the sunset flames', the solitary

tree which the two young Oxford men had prized, saying
that, as long as it stood, their friend the Scholar-Gipsy
would still be roaming the countryside. Revisiting the
Cumnor hills after Thyrsis' death, the poet searches for
it in vain until, flying from a 'troop of Oxford hunters'
like the Scholar-Gipsy before him, he suddenly sees,

> Back'd by the sunset, which doth glorify
> The orange and pale violet evening-sky,
> Bare on its lonely ridge, the Tree! the Tree!

At the end of the poem, he recognizes that he is now
obliged to live amid 'city-noise'. But he hopes that
'through the great town's harsh, heart-wearying roar'
Thyrsis' voice will come to him, driving away 'fatigue
and fear':

> *Why faintest thou? I wander'd till I died.*
> *Roam on! The light we sought is shining still.*
> *Dost thou ask proof? Our tree yet crowns the hill,*
> *Our Scholar travels yet the loved hill-side.*

So the poem ends on a note of optimism. Just as
Arnold in 'Obermann Once More', probably written in
1865-6, repudiates the defeatism of 'Stanzas in Memory
of the Author of *Obermann*', written at least in part in
1849, so he clearly intended that 'Thyrsis' should differ
from 'The Scholar-Gipsy' in expressing a hopeful acceptance of the obligation to participate in 'modern life'.
In his prose writings of this time can be found his reasons
for feeling this temperate but genuine hopefulness. In
his poetry its expression carries very much less weight.
In 'Obermann Once More' it is merely asserted. In
'Thyrsis' it is more skilfully suggested by means of the
symbolism of the tree. But does not even this seem to be
rather too deliberately introduced?

Much more persuasive is the expression of his melancholy longing for 'The years that are no more' ('Growing
Old'). 'Thyrsis', like 'The Scholar-Gipsy', is memorable
chiefly for its vivid, almost Keatsian recreation of the
well-loved Cumnor landscape. This is so presented as
potently to suggest by its details the coolness, freshness,
and seclusion for which the poet yearned.

Containing this achievement, the Oxford elegies are
poems of charm and distinction. But they are too far
removed from the harsh exigencies of life for it to be
easy to claim greatness for them. Arnold has himself
supplied the criterion, 'Dover Beach', by reference to
which this becomes apparent. Admittedly, the stresses
and clashes of life are acknowledged in the poems; but
they are much less concretely present there than is the
idyllic landscape to which the poet flies from them. Nor
is the 'quest' which inspires this revisiting of places long
loved made any more real to us. What we are offered is
a brief escape from the human predicament 'on the view-
less wings of Poesy'. There are times when we are glad
to make such an escape. But the fact remains that the
greatest poetry is that which confronts and in some sense
masters the predicament.

VI

Several conclusions emerge from what has been said
so far. The most important of these is that Arnold
achieves poetic greatness only on one or two exceptional,
Empedoclean occasions. When in early life he tried to
protect himself by dandyism against those who might
accentuate his tendency towards depth-hunting, he was
probably doing what was most conducive to his own
eventual personal happiness; but it would seem that he

was denying himself the material best suited to his creative talent. In keeping with this programme, he tried to cultivate in his poetry the calm, cheerfulness, and disinterested objectivity which he ascribed to the early Greek genius; but the best of what I should call his Calliclean poems are what they are rather because they give moving expression to an essentially personal impulse of escape than because they embody with entire assurance the early Greek virtues he admired. There are three long works, however, in which he very deliberately attempted to realize these classical qualities without subjective adulteration. These are 'Sohrab and Rustum', 'Balder Dead', and *Merope*. 'Balder Dead' is tame, and *Merope* is almost unreadable; but 'Sohrab and Rustum' is a work of sufficient power to claim attention both for itself and for the critical theories associated with it.

These theories are expounded in the 'Preface' to his *Poems* of 1853. They clearly derive from views which we have already met in his letters to Clough. In the 'Preface', after explaining why he has suppressed 'Empedocles on Etna', he goes on to repeat that his condemnation of it was not due to its dealing with a subject belonging to a distant time and country. Critics are wrong, he says, to urge poets to forsake such subjects in favour of modern ones. An action which is excellent for poetic purposes may be either modern or ancient. In either case, however, it must be such as to appeal powerfully 'to the great primary human affections: to those elementary feelings which subsist permanently in the race, and which are independent of time.' Even so, poets should remember that the Greeks, 'with their exquisite sagacity of taste', felt that a modern action was 'too much mixed up with what was accidental and passing, to form a sufficiently grand, detached, and self-subsistent object for a tragic poem'; such an action, they felt, would be more appropriately treated in lighter verse.

So the poet must above all choose an excellent action for his poem, rejecting the advice of those who would, by encouraging him to make his poem a 'true allegory of the state' of his 'own mind', foster a romantic subjectivism in him. Arnold urges him to frequent the ancients, for they can teach him three indispensable things: 'the all-importance of the choice of a subject; the necessity of accurate construction; and the subordinate character of expression'. In practice, nineteenth-century critics deny the third of these and ignore the other two. 'They will permit the Poet to select any action he pleases, and to suffer that action to go as it will, provided he gratifies them with occasional bursts of fine writing, and with a shower of isolated thoughts and images.' The influence even of Shakespeare himself can help to seduce a poet into this heresy. So, too, can that of Keats, despite his 'exquisite genius'. While Arnold nowhere mentions any living English poet in this 'Preface', it seems likely that he had in mind, as a contemporary who had been so seduced, the 'Spasmodic' Alexander Smith, the first of whose volumes of verse had appeared earlier in 1853.

In an 'Advertisement' to the second edition of his *Poems*, published in 1854, Arnold acknowledged that his doctrines were not directly applicable to lyric poetry. Of the three works which he attempted to write in accordance with them, two, 'Sohrab and Rustum' and 'Balder Dead', are in the epic manner, and the third, *Merope*, is a tragedy.

'Sohrab and Rustum' appears as 'The Death of Sohrab' in a list of projected poems which Arnold drew up probably in 1851. It is likely that he made slow progress with

it at first. Then, in April 1853, he was able to tell Jane
that he was writing 'a thing that gives me more pleasure
than anything I have ever done yet, which is a good sign'.
But school-inspection meant grievous interruptions; and
'whether I shall not ultimately spoil it by being obliged
to strike it off in fragments, instead of at one heat, I
cannot quite say'. He finished the poem by May 1 and
wrote to Clough and to his mother saying that he thought
it the best thing he had yet done.

He had originally met the 'very noble and excellent'
story in an essay of Sainte-Beuve's. Sir John Malcolm's
History of Persia had then given him further information;
Sir Alexander Burnes' *Travels into Bokhara* had helped
him to orientalize the poem; and, as was consistent with
the programme he was subsequently to draw up in his
'Preface', he had leaned heavily on Homer in attempting
to give the work an epic quality.

It would not be grossly unjust to call 'Sohrab and
Rustum' a superbly accomplished piece of academic
verse. Its dignity, genuine but rather self-conscious, is
the product of a deliberate design to present an excellent
action worthily in the Homeric style. Arnold himself
suspected that his verse had not the rapidity, though he
hoped that it had the fluidity, of Homer's; eventually, he
came to think it too Miltonic. Moreover, twenty-two
developed similes are rather more than Homer would
easily have allowed himself in a passage of fewer than
nine hundred lines; it may be that, in introducing so
many, Arnold was succumbing to some extent to the very
heresy which he denounced in his 'Preface'. But in the
main his poem is Homeric enough.

Twice at least it transcends mere literary virtuosity.
The fight between the father and the son, like that on
the 'darkling plain', is fought between 'ignorant'

opponents—ignorant in this instance of the relationship
which binds them.

> And you would say that sun and stars took part
> In that unnatural conflict; for a cloud
> Grew suddenly in Heaven, and dark'd the sun
> Over the fighters' heads; and a wind rose
> Under their feet, and moaning swept the plain,
> And in a sandy whirlwind wrapp'd the pair.
> In gloom they twain were wrapp'd, and they alone;
> For both the on-looking hosts on either hand
> Stood in broad daylight, and the sky was pure,
> And the sun sparkled on the Oxus stream.

During an interval, Sohrab proposes peace to his 'fierce'
father. Rustum retorts:

> Girl! nimble with thy feet, not with thy hands!
> Curl'd minion, dancer, coiner of sweet words!

Is it fanciful to hear in these lines the voice of Dr. Arnold
reproving the flippancy of young Matthew? Psychological
criticism is often absurdly irrelevant, but in this instance
a psychological explanation does seem to be called for.
'Sohrab and Rustum' is, I suggest, from one point of view
an imaginative projection of the conflict between Arnold
and his formidable father who had died over ten years
earlier. From this source, unrecognized presumably by
Arnold himself, it derives much of the power which
distinguishes it from the more completely objective
'Balder Dead' and *Merope*.

As is natural, this power is most evident at the climax
of the poem, in the description of the fight. In detail,
this is Homeric. But Arnold has sharply visualized the
whole affair, and he presents it directly, exactly, and
vividly. Similes, elsewhere often very fully—and sometimes very charmingly—developed, are here forbidden

to run beyond three or four lines each; and the language has an economy and a force frequently lacking in the long speeches which make up so much of the rest of the poem.

The reference to 'the Oxus stream', in the passage quoted, is one of many which, from the second line of 'Sohrab and Rustum' onwards, prepare us for the fuller description of the river which forms a coda to the episode. In his letters, Arnold repeatedly voices the 'perfect passion for clear water' which he may well have caught from his father. In his poetic landscapes, not only mountains but also streams and the sea have important places. Again and again he writes of the river of life or time and of the sea of eternity; 'The Future' is a conspicuous instance. In 'Sohrab and Rustum' the Oxus is never explicitly identified with the river of life. But no reader of the poem is likely to deny that it is so conceived in the concluding lines; and that its constant presence is largely responsible for the sense of fatality which broods over the whole work. In this last paragraph there is still much of literary virtuosity—the evocative use of resonant and exotic proper names, for example; nevertheless, the lines do constitute the second important region in which the poem transcends calculable achievement.

> But the majestic river floated on,
> Out of the mist and hum of that low land,
> Into the frosty starlight, and there moved,
> Rejoicing, through the hush'd Chorasmian waste,
> Under the solitary moon;—he flow'd
> Right for the polar star, past Orgunjè,
> Brimming, and bright, and large; then sands begin
> To hem his watery march, and dam his streams,
> And split his currents; that for many a league

The shorn and parcell'd Oxus strains along
Through beds of sand and matted rushy isles—
Oxus, forgetting the bright speed he had
In his high mountain-cradle in Pamere,
A foil'd circuitous wanderer—till at last
The long'd-for dash of waves is heard, and wide
His luminous home of waters opens, bright
And tranquil, from whose floor the new-bathed stars
Emerge, and shine upon the Aral Sea.

Describing how father and son were destined to engage
each other in a single combat ending with the son's loss
of 'youth, and bloom, and this delightful world',
'Sohrab and Rustum' is unmistakably a work which at
certain points engaged its author's deepest personal feelings. To this, I have suggested, it owes its superiority to
'Balder Dead' and *Merope*. Arnold's attempts to select
excellent actions such as would appeal 'to those elementary feelings which subsist permanently in the race, and
which are independent of time', were quite misguided.
It may well be a true critical observation that such
actions excel those which appeal only to what is 'accidental and passing'. But is the criterion one which can be
safely employed by the poet himself? If it induces him to
prefer to a subject which interests him personally another
which his critical intelligence tells him is superior but
which interests him less, is the result not likely to be
precisely the frigid academic versifying which we find in
'Balder Dead' and *Merope*? From the fate of these
'Sohrab and Rustum' was saved by the fact that in this
instance the excellent action was also one which mat-
tered a great deal more to the poet himself than he knew.
It is easy to sympathize with Arnold's wish to avoid
the undisciplined subjectivism of certain of his contemporaries and immediate predecessors. But he attempted

too entire an exclusion of subjective factors from the works with which we are now concerned. His artistic success, complete or partial, absolute or relative, in those poems in which he most relied upon symbolic landscapes—Dover, Berkshire, the Oxus—suggests that symbolism offered him the best possible opportunity of concentrating upon the presentation and grouping of objects while not denying himself the power which could only come from the full enlistment of his deepest personal feelings. But Arnold, though in many ways an excellent critic of his own work, did not admit this suggestion. As a result, too much of his work consists of uncreative ruminations and academic exercises. His good poems are regrettably few. Only once did he fully exploit a symbolic landscape in the service of his deeper, Empedoclean impulse; and on that occasion he wrote his one great poem, 'Dover Beach'.

THE CRITIC

I

ARNOLD gave his inaugural address as Professor of Poetry on 14 November 1857. During the following ten years, he published three volumes of literary criticism. The first and third of these, *On Translating Homer* (1861) and *On the Study of Celtic Literature* (1867), contained two series of Oxford lectures, delivered in 1860–1 and 1865–6. The second, *Essays in Criticism* (1865), was very largely a miscellany of lectures given at Oxford during the intervening period.

In 1869, after he had relinquished the Professorship, Arnold allowed his inaugural address, 'On the Modern Element in Literature', to be printed in a magazine. In this, he describes the modern spirit as the spirit of those who, aware of a rich past and a complex present, desire above all to understand their situation, to achieve a rational appreciation of the facts. It is this spirit of disinterested enquiry that he tries to serve in his literary, political, and religious criticism.

(i)

In his Homer lectures, he studies the chief existing translations of the *Iliad* with a view to giving practical advice to future translators. He distinguishes four main qualities of Homer's poetry: its flowing rapidity of movement, its simplicity of style, its plainness of thought, and, above all, its nobility. He finds that Cowper loses

Homer's rapidity of movement, because he employs an
elaborate Miltonic style; that Pope's literary artificial
manner is utterly opposed to the requisite simplicity;
and that Chapman replaces Homer's plainness of thought
by an Elizabethan fancifulness. There can be no doubt
about the talents of these translators; nevertheless, none
of them has successfully reproduced all four of the essential Homeric qualities. But much worse than their failure
is that of Francis W. Newman.

When this younger brother of the future Cardinal
published his rendering of the *Iliad*, he was Professor of
Latin at University College, London. His intellectual
powers and his erudition were great; but he was ludi-
crously deficient in common sense, in humour, and in
judgment. He was a rationalist, a faddist, a pedant, and
an eccentric.

He made it clear that he had his own way of seeing
Homer's poetry. He found it, like the old English
ballads, 'direct, popular, forcible, quaint, flowing,
garrulous'; and he held that, when the subject allowed
it, Homer's verse could be 'prosaic' or 'low'. Arnold
extracts and exhibits the words 'quaint', 'garrulous',
'prosaic', and 'low' as evidence of Newman's utter misconception of his task.

Newman's performance is faithful to his misconception. His translation is couched in an absurd and barbarous jargon which may be fairly represented by such
phrases as 'dapper-greav'd Achaians' and such lines as

Nor liefly thee would I advance to man-ennobling battle.

This rendering is the disastrous failure that it is, says
Arnold, because it has nothing of the fourth and most
important of the main qualities of Homer's poetry: it is
without nobility. Even Newman's metrical form, based

upon that usual in the old English ballads, is incompatible with the achievement of 'the grand style'.

Arnold had alluded to 'the *grand style*' in the 'Preface' of 1853; he now attempts to clarify his meaning. He does not try to define it in abstract terms; 'that sort of general discussion', he says, 'never much helps our judgment of particular instances.' Instead, he adopts a procedure which he has already used more than once and which he will often use again. Just as a few flat lines from a medieval romance have served to convey what he understands by the 'garrulity' which Newman wrongheadedly ascribes to Homer, so he now explains himself by quoting concrete examples of the grand style from Homer, Virgil, Dante, and Milton.

This nobility, this grand style, can do more than merely touch and stir the feelings; 'it can form the character, it is edifying'. Conversely, the achievement of it depends upon certain qualities of character in the writer. Naturally, Arnold cannot with decency emphasize this dependence while publicly condemning as ignoble the work of a living author; but he mentions it, without overt reference to Newman, twice.

What he does develop more fully at the end of his second lecture is the view that the eccentricity and arbitrariness exemplified by Newman's misconception of Homer are not peculiar to Newman himself; they are 'the great defect of English intellect, the great blemish of English literature'. The English admit readily enough that there is a right and wrong in matters of conduct; but they cannot see that there is equally a right and wrong in matters of intellect and taste. The exercise of the critical spirit, with its aim 'in all branches of knowledge—theology, philosophy, history, art, science—to see the object as in itself it really is' could do much to enlighten

I

them. But the inferiority of contemporary English literature to contemporary French and German literature is
due precisely to the weakness in it of this modern, critical
spirit. Arnold hopes eventually to strengthen it and by
so doing to stimulate the growth of an intellectual
conscience among his fellow-countrymen. For a start,
he sets up an imaginary tribunal of classical scholars of
poetic sensibility as an embodiment of the true and
impersonal standards of judgment by which he condemns
Newman's translation.

His comments upon this did not go unanswered. He
had marvelled at the fantastic diction which Newman had
compiled with the avowed intention of being moderately
archaic but easily intelligible. 'Where, indeed, Mr.
Newman got his diction, with whom he can have lived,
what can be his test of antiquity and rarity for words,
are questions which I ask myself with bewilderment.'
The *Saturday Review* retorted pointedly that 'at one time
at least of his life, he "lived with" the other Fellows
of Balliol, and that his academical honours were considerably higher than those of the present Poetry Professor'.
Newman himself, in *Homeric Translation in Theory and
Practice* (1861), solemnly complained that he was being
accused 'of keeping low company'! In this counterblast
to Arnold's original series of lectures, Newman's greater
erudition sometimes gives him the advantage. But whenever he quotes from his own version he spoils his case.
Nothing like Newman's freakish and pedantic synthetic
jargon was ever used either by Homer or by any other
poet of distinction.

In *Last Words on Translating Homer* (1862), Arnold
amplifies and develops his earlier criticism of English
intellect. He argues that Newman could hardly have
persisted in his eccentric and arbitrary misconception of

Homer if there had existed in England 'a public force of correct literary opinion' such as is embodied in, and promoted by, the French Academy. As things are, a misconception of this kind is more likely to lead others astray than to undergo correction itself. So anyone 'who can introduce a little order into this chaos by establishing in any quarter a single sound rule of criticism, a single rule which clearly marks what is right as right, and what is wrong as wrong, does a good deed'. Not that he can be sure that he has fixed any such rule. A belief in the validity of standards of criticism is far from guaranteeing an infallible knowledge of them. But in Europe in the long run, if not in the critic's own nation immediately, 'there is a final judgment on these matters, and the critic's work will at last stand or fall by its true merits'.

By a 'sound rule' Arnold here means a trustworthy guiding principle, not an inflexible and tyrannical law. In the original series of lectures, for example, he suggests that a translator of Homer who is in doubt whether a particular word is plain and noble enough for his purpose can obtain useful guidance by ascertaining whether it is or is not used in the Authorized Version of the Bible. Newman takes this to mean that if a word is not in the Bible it is ignoble. Arnold deplores such heavyhandedness. 'Nothing of the kind: there are no such absolute rules to be laid down in these matters.'

In the same spirit, he deprecates 'that obduracy and over-vehemence in liking and disliking,—a remnant, I suppose, of our insular ferocity,—to which English criticism is so prone'. As a disciple of Sainte-Beuve, he sees clearly the need for pliancy and suppleness—qualities which learning such as Newman's can only too easily damage in its possessor. 'The critic of poetry should have the finest tact, the nicest moderation, the most free,

flexible, and elastic spirit imaginable; he should be
indeed the "ondoyant et divers," the *undulating and
diverse* being of Montaigne.' Above all, he should be
eagerly receptive. In agreement with some of his greatest
predecessors—Dryden, Addison, Johnson, and Coleridge
for example—Arnold declares that 'it is the critic's first
duty,—prior even to his duty of stigmatising what is bad
—*to welcome everything that is good*'.

What we have in these passages is a draft of Arnold's
programme at the outset of his career as a critic. In
intention, his criticism is to be adaptable, open-minded,
and enquiring. It is to promote the acknowledgment
of true and impersonal standards of judgment. It is to
concern itself as much as possible with particular works
and as little as possible with general rules and defini-
tions.

Critics of the original series of lectures drove him to
depart from the last of these resolutions so far as to
attempt a formal definition of 'the grand style'. He
decides that this 'arises in poetry, *when a noble nature,
poetically gifted, treats with simplicity or with severity a
serious subject*'. But so much, and more, we have already
learned from his concrete instances of the grand style
in Shakespeare, Milton, and others.

Elsewhere, Arnold's determination to keep fresh both
his own and his reader's sense of the actual poetry with
which he is concerned, coupled with his declared aim of
giving practical advice to aspiring translators of Homer,
leads to a good deal of detailed literary analysis. In fact,
the Homer lectures contain much of his finest criticism
of this sort.

The third lecture, for example, includes a demonstra-
tion that Miltonic blank verse is unsuitable for a translation of Homer because its movement is 'a laboured, a

self-retarding movement'. Arnold analyses this 'un-Homeric effect' with care. In *Last Words* he analyses with even greater care another un-Homeric effect when he replies to a critic's contention that Tennyson's blank verse has a Greek plainness of thought and simplicity of expression. He insists that, whereas Homer gives us 'natural thoughts in natural words', Tennyson gives us 'distilled thoughts in distilled words'. Even when Tennyson tries to be simple he attains not the real quality but only a semblance of it, not *simplicité* but *simplesse*. A comparison of representative passages by Wordsworth and Tennyson supports this judgment.

Among much else that is admirable about Arnold's method in these critiques, his use of quotation calls for particular notice. Passages are well chosen; and the commentary in which they are set is skilfully designed so to launch us upon our reading of them that we are naturally led to perceive the qualities for which Arnold has included them. The more we see for ourselves, the less Arnold needs to tell us; in this way, detailed analysis is achieved without his subjecting us to the paralysing torture of scrupulous explication.

The tone, too, calls for praise. Arnold was aware that any adverse comments by a poet upon a living colleague were only too likely to be attributed to odious motives. For this reason, he normally avoided publishing criticism of contemporary writers. But in his remarks on Tennyson he manages with consummate tact first to place Tennyson relatively to Homer and then to place certain of his poems relatively to certain of Wordsworth's. While Tennyson suffers by each comparison, Arnold very promptly acknowledges the distinction and charm of his work and concedes parenthetically that even *simplesse* can be 'very beautiful and valuable'. The amenity and urbanity of this are most engaging. Arnold's charm could sometimes seem rather deliberately applied; but here his manner is impeccable, his poise perfect.

(ii)

It is clear that Arnold set himself as a critic two tasks which have not always been thought compatible with each other. He wished to preserve the utmost flexibility and receptiveness in his approach to literature; but, at the same time, he felt it his duty to testify to the authority of intellectual and aesthetic standards. The one aim links him with romantic critics such as Hazlitt and Pater, the other with classicists such as Johnson. His first series[1] of *Essays in Criticism* opens with two Oxford lectures in which he reviews these aims in turn.

'The Function of Criticism at the Present Time' begins with a reply to those who complained that the author of the lectures *On Translating Homer* over-rated criticism. Arnold grants that criticism is inferior to creation. But, he argues, the creation of great works of art is not always equally possible. Even the tremendous natural powers of the Romantics were partially crippled by the lack, in the English society of the nineteenth century, of a vigorous intellectual life such as had upheld more fortunate poets. 'This makes Byron so empty of matter, Shelley so incoherent, Wordsworth even, profound as he is, yet so wanting in completeness and variety.' The deficiency is one which criticism can help to remedy. In fact, criticism can be of incalculable service to future creative writers merely by performing its true business. 'Its business is . . . simply to know the best that is known and thought in the world, and by in its turn making this

---

[1] So called to distinguish it from the further series published after his death.

known, to create a current of true and fresh ideas.' It tends in this way to produce eventually an intellectual and spiritual atmosphere by which creative genius can be happily inspired.

If it is to be successful, criticism must be essentially the exercise of curiosity, in the best sense of that word. Moreover, it must be disinterested; it must steadily refuse to lend itself to 'ulterior, political, practical considerations'. While the practical man tends to see an object only in so far as it seems likely to aid or impede his designs, the critic must try to view it more detachedly, to see it 'as in itself it really is'.

Criticism, so conceived, is to be directed not only upon works of art but also upon life in general. Arnold himself in this essay directs it upon passages from two recent political speeches complacently celebrating the greatness of the English race and its achievements. Dismissing as irrelevant to his purpose the particular practical ends which the speakers may have been trying to secure by their rhapsodies, and which therefore he may be helping to thwart by his criticism, he points out that 'there is a peril for poor human nature in words and thoughts of such exuberant self-satisfaction'. He shows up what is excessive and offensive in the dithyrambs by juxtaposing with them a brutally compact newspaper report of a squalid child-murder recently committed in the very country which they extol. This is the comparative method already used with skill in his criticisms of Milton and Tennyson. For Arnold maintains that the habit of dispassionate appraisal fostered by strictly literary criticism can be of the widest social utility. He upholds the value to the community of the flexible, non-specialist intelligence.

Yet a critic of this kind is very likely to be misunderstood. In England, where 'practice is everything, a free play of the mind is nothing', such misunderstanding is almost inevitable, especially where politics and religion are concerned.

For here people are particularly indisposed even to comprehend that without this free disinterested treatment of things, truth and the highest culture are out of the question. So immersed are they in practical life, so accustomed to take all their notions from this life and its processes, that they are apt to think that truth and culture themselves can be reached by the processes of this life, and that it is an impertinent singularity to think of reaching them in any other. 'We are all *terrae filii*,' cries their eloquent advocate; 'all Philistines together. Away with the notion of proceeding by any other course than the course dear to the Philistines; let us have a social movement, let us organise and combine a party to pursue truth and new thought, let us call it *the liberal party*, and let us all stick to each other, and back each other up. Let us have no nonsense about independent criticism, and intellectual delicacy, and the few and the many. Don't let us trouble ourselves about foreign thought; we shall invent the whole thing for ourselves as we go along. If one of us speaks well, applaud him; if one of us speaks ill, applaud him too; we are all in the same movement, we are all liberals, we are all in pursuit of truth.' In this way the pursuit of truth becomes really a social, practical, pleasurable affair, almost requiring a chairman, a secretary, and advertisements; with the excitement of an occasional scandal, with a little resistance to give the happy sense of difficulty overcome; but, in general, plenty of bustle and very little thought. To act is so easy, as Goethe says; to think is so hard! It is true that the critic has many temptations to go with the stream, to make one of the party movement, one of these *terrae filii*; it seems ungracious to refuse to be a *terrae filius*, when so many excellent people are; but the critic's duty is to refuse, or, if resistance is vain, at least to cry with Obermann: *Périssons en résistant*.

Here, as elsewhere, Arnold's banter and irony enable him to attack without loss of poise. Caricature, too, was to remain a favourite weapon with him.

He concludes the essay with a few recommendations for strictly literary criticism. This, he repeats, should be the exercise of disinterested curiosity. Admittedly, 'judging is often spoken of as the critic's one business, and so in some sense it is; but the judgment which almost insensibly forms itself in a fair and clear mind, along with fresh knowledge, is the valuable one'. When deliberate judgment is called for, 'the great safeguard is never to let oneself become abstract, always to retain an intimate and lively consciousness of the truth of what one is saying, and, the moment this fails us, to be sure that something is wrong'.

In his search for 'the best that is known and thought', the English critic will need to dwell much on foreign literature. What, in fact, really interests Arnold is a criticism 'which regards Europe as being, for intellectual and spiritual purposes, one great confederation, bound to a joint action and working to a common result; and whose members have, for their proper outfit, a knowledge of Greek, Roman, and Eastern antiquity, and of one another.' This European ideal had been Goethe's.

I have quoted here only a few of the very many shrewd judgments and wise recommendations which distinguish this, perhaps the finest essay Arnold ever wrote. The idea of a criticism which will be 'sincere, simple, flexible, ardent, ever widening its knowledge' is an inspiring one. To say that Arnold did not fully realize it in his own work is merely to admit human imperfection. No one has ever fully realized it. Among the reasons why Arnold is one of our great critics are, firstly, that he did, to a remarkable degree, make his criticism an expression of disinterested curiosity and, secondly, that he clearly perceived that the critical attitude is of value not only in the writer's or reader's study but also in the world outside.

But what of the standards by which 'the best that is known and thought' is to be recognized? Prudently, Arnold refrains on the whole from abstract definition. For him, the standards are embodied in the works of Homer, Dante, Shakespeare, Goethe, and others. In England, however, their existence is commonly either ignored or denied; and from this certain inconveniences follow. These inconveniences are the main subject of the second of the *Essays in Criticism*, 'The Literary Influence of Academies'.

A short historical account of the establishment of the French Academy as 'a high court of letters', 'a recognised authority, imposing . . . a high standard in matters of intellect and taste', introduces the main theme of this essay. The French have set up such an authority because they possess a sensitiveness of intellectual conscience which makes them feel its desirability. The English have done nothing of the kind.

The implication is obvious. But Arnold draws it only with the greatest delicacy and circumspection. The English, he grants readily enough, have energy and honesty. Even in the aesthetic and intellectual fields, this energy has enabled them to do remarkable things; their poets and scientists include men of the most astonishing imaginative genius, men such as Shakespeare and Newton. But, in any undertaking which calls less for the creative energy of genius than for an open mind and a flexible intelligence, their performance is decidedly weaker. In short, they suffer from a lack of the critical spirit. Even their finest achievement, their poetry, is deficient in the things which this can give, for example, 'form, method, precision, proportions, arrangement'. In prose, where such things are all-important, they lag far behind the French, in whom the critical spirit is strong. Creative energy is presumably inborn; the critical spirit, on the other hand, can be considerably fostered by such an institution as its own child, the French Academy.

This 'sets standards in a number of directions, and creates, in all these directions, a force of educated opinion, checking and rebuking those who fall below these standards, or who set them at nought'. Uncontrolled by any force of opinion of this kind, English intellect expends itself in works such as F. W. Newman's *Iliad*; it becomes guilty of 'hap-hazard, crudeness, provincialism, eccentricity, violence, blundering'.

One of these sins, provincialism, is Arnold's main topic in the latter part of the essay. He quotes passages from 'our greatest English prose-writer', Edmund Burke, and comments that they are written in extravagant, capricious, provincial prose. 'People may reply, it is rich and imaginative; yes, that is just it, it is *Asiatic* prose, as the ancient critics would have said; prose somewhat barbarously rich and over-loaded. But the true prose is Attic prose.' For modern Attic prose, he looks to France.

To provinciality he opposes urbanity, a quality which he finds in the prose of J. H. Newman but very rarely elsewhere in English.

The provincial spirit . . . exaggerates the value of its ideas for want of a high standard at hand by which to try them. Or rather, for want of such a standard, it gives one idea too much prominence at the expense of others; it orders its ideas amiss; it is hurried away by fancies; it likes and dislikes too passionately, too exclusively. Its admiration weeps hysterical tears, and its disapprobation foams at the mouth. So we get the *eruptive* and the *aggressive* manner in literature; the former prevails most in our criticism, the latter in our newspapers. For, not having the lucidity of a large and centrally placed intelligence, the provincial spirit has not its graciousness; it does not persuade, it makes war; it has not urbanity, the tone of the city, of the centre, the tone which always aims at a spiritual and intellectual effect, and not excluding the use of banter, never disjoins banter itself from politeness, from felicity. But the provincial tone is more violent, and seems to aim rather at an effect upon the blood and senses than upon the spirit and intellect; it loves hard-hitting rather than persuading. The newspaper, with its party spirit, its thorough-goingness, its resolute avoidance of shades and distinctions, its short, highly-charged, heavy-shotted articles, its style so unlike that style *lenis minimèque pertinax*—easy and not too violently insisting,—which the ancients so much admired, is its true literature.

Even writers of rare talent, he continues, are more or less disabled in England by their remoteness from 'a supposed centre of correct information, correct judgment, correct taste'. John Ruskin, for example, has written a great deal of extraordinarily beautiful, almost poetic, descriptive prose. This is the product of his genius, of 'the original and incommunicable part' in him. But when he is exercising his intelligence and judgment, 'the acquired, trained, communicable part in him', he is only too liable to produce extravagant fantasticalities such as his speculation, which Arnold quotes, on the esoteric significance of the names of Shakespeare's characters. F. T. Palgrave, similarly, whose *Golden Treasury* shows his 'very fine critical tact', can be guilty of 'freaks and violences', both in the notes to that anthology and elsewhere, which would probably be impossible to him if he were not in this country too much left to take his own way.

In each of these short critiques, as in that on Tennyson considered earlier, Arnold takes care that his strictures are accompanied by an acknowledgment of the genuine ability of the author in question. He does not wish to give one part of the truth too much prominence at the expense of others; he does not wish to like and dislike too passionately, too exclusively. He wishes to possess 'urbanity, the tone of the city, of the centre'.

With A. W. Kinglake, the historian of the Crimean War, he is more severe. Arnold acknowledges his 'really eminent' talent but states that he writes in the Corinthian style. This is the style of a good editorial. It is inferior to the Attic and even to the Asiatic style; 'it has glitter without warmth, rapidity without ease, effectiveness without charm. Its characteristic is, that it has no *soul*; all it exists for, is to get its ends, to make its points, to damage its adversaries, to be admired, to triumph. A style so bent on effect at the expense of soul, simplicity, and delicacy; a style so little studious of the charm of the great models; so far from classic truth and grace, must surely be said to have the note of provinciality.' Elsewhere, several brief descriptions of Macaulay's prose show that in Arnold's eyes this, too, was Corinthian.

In England, then, it is almost impossible to redeem oneself from provinciality. Inadvertently, Arnold himself illustrates the difficulty. For is there not something provincial in his considered display of his own delicacy, moderation, and urbanity? Accused, he would probably have referred once more to the inconveniences associated with the lack of an academy.

Yet it would be provincial to allow even an admiration for the French Academy to become obsessional. So,

after all that he has said in its favour, Arnold turns round
and admits that an academy may be injuriously repressive.
But, he adds, 'this side of the question it rather behoves
the French, not us, to study'. For it is an important part
of the function of criticism, as Arnold sees it, to emphasize those aspects of the truth which are most likely to
be overlooked by the people whom it addresses.

The conclusion is hardly that which his more practically minded readers must have expected. In the spirit
of Burke, he advises against the establishment of an
academy in this country, on the grounds that it would
be contrary to the whole national tradition. As a disinterested critic, he does not aim directly at practice;
he wishes merely to promote dispassionate reflection on
the subject of academies. By so doing he hopes to make
his readers more keenly aware of the shortcomings and
excesses to which, in the absence of a sovereign organ of
opinion, they are especially liable. Everyone with any
turn for literature, he says, 'will do well constantly to
try himself in respect of these, steadily to widen his
culture, severely to check in himself the provincial
spirit; and he will do this the better the more he keeps
in mind that all mere glorification by ourselves of ourselves or our literature . . . is both vulgar, and, besides
being vulgar, retarding.'

After this, he might reasonably have supposed that he
would not be accused of trying to introduce in England
an institution like the French Academy. Nevertheless,
the accusation was made; and his retort to it, in the
'Preface' to *Culture and Anarchy*, is a lively satirical flight
of fancy. In his mind's eye, he sees 'everything which is
influential, accomplished, and distinguished' enrolled in
'the happy family', the English Academy; 'and then,
some fine morning, a dissatisfaction of the public mind

with this brilliant and select coterie, a flight of Corinthian leading articles, and an irruption of Mr. G. A. Sala.[1] Clearly, this is not what will do us good. The very same faults,—the want of sensitiveness of intellectual conscience, the disbelief in right reason, the dislike of authority,—which have hindered our having an Academy and have worked injuriously in our literature, would also hinder us from making our Academy, if we established it, one which would really correct them.'

Throughout his career as a critic, Arnold's conception of his task was essentially that expounded in these two lectures. The remainder of *Essays in Criticism* illustrates it further.

He insists, for example, that the English critic should dwell much on foreign literature; so none of these essays deals primarily with an English author. Nor is this the only way in which he combats the 'genuine British narrowness'. His essay on Heine, from whom he quotes this phrase, contains a direct assault upon it.

Describing Heine as an apostle of the modern spirit, Arnold develops the account of that spirit given in his inaugural address. Modern Europe, he says, has inherited from feudal times 'an immense system of institutions, established facts, accredited dogmas, customs, rules', which does not correspond with its actual needs. The modern spirit awakens whenever and wherever this lack of correspondence is perceived. It is now awake almost everywhere. The old European order must be dissolved; 'what we have to study is that we may not be acrid dissolvents of it'. Goethe's example is instructive. His 'profound, imperturbable naturalism' tends irresistibly to sap all routine thinking. Heine, however, more impatient, shouts a desperate defiance of 'the Philistines'.

---

[1] A well-known journalist on the staff of the *Daily Telegraph*.

We have already seen Arnold apply this term in 'The Function of Criticism at the Present Time' to the '*terrae filii*'; but the essay on Heine is of slightly earlier date, and it is there that he introduces the German nickname into the English language. He defines a 'Philistine' as 'a strong, dogged, unenlightened opponent of the chosen people, of the children of the light' and explains that the German representatives of the modern spirit saw themselves 'as children of the light' and saw their adversaries 'as humdrum people, slaves to routine, enemies to light; stupid and oppressive, but at the same time very strong'. For his part, Arnold decides that England is 'the very head-quarters of Goliath'.

There, at the beginning of the nineteenth century, Byron and Shelley tried to write, like Goethe and Heine, as representatives of the modern spirit. They failed. The 'resistance to baffle them, the want of intelligent sympathy to guide and uphold them, were too great'. Less ambitious writers—Wordsworth, Scott, and Keats, for example—were more successful. This verdict on the English Romantics underlies that already quoted from 'The Function of Criticism at the Present Time'.

In keeping with his declared programme for criticism, Arnold tries in this volume to stimulate a free play of the mind upon various stock notions and prejudices of the complacent English Philistines. Their anti-Catholicism in particular attracts his notice. In 'Eugénie de Guérin', he compares English Protestantism with French Catholicism and decides that English Protestantism gives to its religious life a setting which is deficient in grace and charm. In 'Pagan and Mediaeval Religious Sentiment' he reminds his readers of 'the rich treasures of human life' which have been stored within the pale of the Catholic Church.

This essay is a good example of Arnold's tactics as a critic. As it develops, it becomes clear that he will not help either Catholicism or Protestantism to repose upon a complacent assumption of its total superiority to its rival; and, when he comes to his main subject, he refuses to allow unqualified merit either to later Hellenic paganism or to mediaeval Christianity. The one lived by the senses and the understanding, the other by the heart and the imagination. Of the two, the latter is the more adequate to the needs of human nature. 'But the main element of the modern spirit's life is neither the senses and understanding, nor the heart and imagination; it is the imaginative reason.'

Arnold's procedure here, as in his discussion of academies, exemplifies the meaning which he attaches to disinterestedness. Criticism is to be exempt from partisan passions, and it is to practise a free play of the mind upon whatever material confronts it.

In 'Pagan and Mediaeval Religious Sentiment', he goes so far as to say, 'I wish to decide nothing as of my own authority; the great art of criticism is to get oneself out of the way and to let humanity decide.' But this is excessive. Before the critic can get out of the way, he will at least have selected and presented the evidence upon which he means humanity to base its decision; and his selection and presentation will themselves tend to influence that decision. If, for instance, he represents English prose by passages from Burke, Ruskin, and Kinglake rather than from Dryden, Swift, and J. H. Newman, he will be insinuating his own belief that English prose is 'provincial', even if he does not, like Arnold, actually state it. This opinion may or may not be correct; my point is merely that Arnold does not refrain from both insinuating and pronouncing it.

K

Clearly, he cannot really intend the critic to abstain from judging. What he does mean is that the judgment should not be founded on practical convenience or partisan prejudice but on as objective an appreciation of the facts as is humanly possible. In a passage already quoted, he states that the valuable judgment is that which almost insensibly forms itself in a fair and clear mind, along with fresh knowledge. The critic fails in disinterestedness not by uttering this judgment which arises from his knowledge but by distorting his knowledge and hence his judgment with a view to the practical consequences of making them known.

Arnold's prose in this volume is brilliantly suited to the purposes of criticism as he understands them. It can be sinuous without meandering; it can be tentative without losing its momentum. It is conversational, polite, and aloof; cool but not frigid; and enlivened repeatedly by a bantering irony. Its mischievous wit is something which we know to have been abundantly present in the man but for which there was, regrettably, no room in his poetry. The ease, grace, and lucidity of this prose make it an admirable medium for the short biographical sketches—those of Maurice and Eugénie de Guérin are especially notable—for which he had so remarkable a gift.

Essays in Criticism was no best-seller; but it excited a good deal of interest, and some opposition, among a small public. In the *Saturday Review*, James Fitzjames Stephen, a Tory utilitarian brother of Leslie Stephen, replied to 'The Function of Criticism at the Present Time' in 1864 and reviewed the whole collection in 1865. In the first of these articles, he complains of Arnold's elevation of the French, from an intellectual and artistic point of view, above the English. He thinks it both unjust and indecent to talk about 'British Philistines'. When the English seem to Arnold to be caring only for immediate practical results, they are really acting on sound Benthamite principles. 'In fact, no nation in the world is so logical as the English nation.' Reviewing *Essays in Criticism*, he observes that the 'Preface' is the work of an offender who is quite unrepentant. It is good-natured, even too good-natured. 'There is no pleasure in hitting a man who will not hit you back again.' Nevertheless, Stephen is determined to argue; and again he enters an earnest and downright protest on behalf of his countrymen.

Stephen was ready enough to praise Arnold's strictly literary criticism. What he resented was the effrontery of a mere man of letters who set up as a 'regenerator of society'. For the same reason, both Dickens and Carlyle elsewhere incurred his ponderous wrath. But Arnold was to persist in acting on his belief that the experienced critic of literature had something valuable to contribute to the discussion of extra-literary matters; and he was again and again in consequence to encounter this sort of opposition.

Arnold took opposition, and even personal insult, with an equanimity unusual among writers. After the *Saturday Review* had published an offensive notice of his Homer lectures, he described his reactions to his mother. 'When first I read a thing of this kind I am annoyed; then I think how certainly in two or three days the effect of it upon me will have wholly passed off; then I begin to think of the openings it gives for observations in answer, and from that moment, when a free activity of the spirit is restored, my gaiety and good spirits return, and the article is simply an object of interest to me.' This was in 1861. He never ceased to be a cheerful and high-spirited controversialist.

(iii)

It cannot be claimed that *On the Study of Celtic Literature*
is among the more important of Arnold's prose works.
But it is unquestionably one of the most attractive of
them. It is a piece of incorrigible amateurism. Owing
to his ignorance of the Celtic languages, Arnold wrote it
without a first-hand acquaintance with its ostensible subject, though the extreme modesty of his pretensions
almost induces the reader to overlook this disability.
What is worse, the argument of the book is erected with
the aid of a scaffolding of now utterly discredited racialist
notions.

Briefly, Arnold's case is that the modern Englishman
unites in himself Norman, Germanic, and Celtic strains.
From his Norman ancestors, he inherits his strenuousness
and his talent for affairs; from the Germanic, his steadi-
ness and his honesty; and, from the Celtic, his ardour and
his sensibility. His problem is fully to realize and to
harmonize in himself the three sets of virtues which these
three strains bring within his reach. By the sympathetic
study of things Celtic, he can foster precisely that set
which he is at present most liable to neglect.

On the Study of Celtic Literature is more than merely
an exercise in an outmoded ideology. Its scientific doctrines are best regarded as so much mythology in terms
of which Arnold found it convenient to express some
acute perceptions and intuitions. These refer mainly to
the Philistines. 'On the side of beauty and taste, vul-
garity; on the side of morals and feeling, coarseness; on
the side of mind and spirit, unintelligence,—this is
Philistinism'; and Philistinism, he feels, is the result
among his fellow-countrymen of too exclusive a reliance

upon the Germanic element in the national make-up. Arnold's aim in this book may be described in the terms which he used in the 'Preface' to its predecessor: 'to pull out a few more stops in that powerful but at present somewhat narrow-toned organ, the modern Englishman'.

His chief interest is in the Celtic stops. He wishes his fellow-countrymen to achieve the heightening and refinement of sensibility which would help to free them from the reproach of being Philistines. Such an achievement is well within their power, since a considerable Celtic heritage has been passed down to them from ancient British forebears. This has been continuously felt in English poetry.

The last section of *On the Study of Celtic Literature* contains Arnold's attempt to demonstrate the truth of this assertion. He thinks it possible that English poetry owes its aptitude for style to a Celtic source. Defining style as 'a peculiar re-casting and heightening, under a certain condition of spiritual excitement, of what a man has to say, in such a manner as to add dignity and distinction to it', he denies it in its fullest development to Goethe, in whom the Germanic nature is unleavened, but recognizes it in Milton. He thinks it probable that English poetry got its 'penetrating passion and melancholy', its Titanism, its impulse to rebel against the despotism of fact, from a Celtic source. In support of this view, he compares a passage from Llywarch Hen with passages from Byron and moves back, *via* Manfred, Lara, and Cain, to Milton's Satan. He thinks it certain, finally, that English poetry is indebted to a Celtic source for its natural magic. 'Magic is just the word for it,— the magic of nature; not merely the beauty of nature, —that the Greeks and Latins had; not merely an honest smack of the soil, a faithful realism,—that the Germans had; but the intimate life of nature, her weird power and her fairy charm.' From Keats and Shakespeare he quotes instances both of 'Greek radiance' and of 'Celtic magic' in the poetic presentation of nature. In fact, he makes more of 'Greek radiance' than is tactically expedient. For, if English poets have succeeded in acquiring this, why must we assume that only inheritance will account for their possession of 'Celtic magic'?

Having praised Celtic poetry for its style, its melancholy, and its natural magic, Arnold, fearful as always of onesidedness, repeats the characteristic manœuvre which we have already observed at the end of his lecture on academies. According to his essay on Maurice de Guérin, the great power of poetry is its interpretative power; and poetry can interpret things and illuminate man both by having natural magic and by having moral profundity. Arnold now turns from the Celts and acknowledges that the Germans, humdrum and prosaic though they may be, have produced a modern poetry which has moral profundity. 'Our great, our only first-rate body of contemporary poetry is the German; the grand business of modern poetry,—a moral interpretation, from an independent point of view, of man and the world,—it is only German poetry, Goethe's poetry, that has, since the Greeks, made much way with.' Arnold's moderation and his 'justness of spirit', as he puts it in his essay on Heine, are attractively exemplified by such returns upon himself as this.

Arnold's attribution of natural magic to Celtic literature has met with general approval. But his view that melancholy is another of its leading characteristics has been widely disputed. It may reasonably be suspected that he owed it to his reading of the eighteenth-century

Ossianic writings of James Macpherson and that he would hardly have arrived at it from a truly dispassionate study of, say, the old Welsh *Mabinogion*. Whatever the grounds for it, however, he undoubtedly succeeded in getting the notion accepted for some time even by professedly Celtic authors. For this reason, he must unquestionably be counted among the precursors of the neo-Ossianic Celtic Renaissance of the quarter-century following his death.

Even during his lifetime, many of those who were working for the preservation of Welsh culture recognized in him a valuable if sometimes severely critical ally. In 1866 he was invited to read a paper at the Welsh national Eisteddfod. He refused because he did not feel qualified to address such a gathering; but he took the opportunity of expressing both his sympathy with the determination of the Welsh to safeguard and honour their language and literature and his admiration for a people with the will to organize Eisteddfodau. His reply was printed in a daily newspaper.

In this way it came to the notice of *The Times*, which, as Arnold says in the 'Preface' to *On the Study of Celtic Literature*, preferred 'a shorter and sharper method of dealing with the Celts'. The 'Thunderer' devoted a leading article to the subject. 'The Welsh language', it ruled, 'is the curse of Wales. Its prevalence, and the ignorance of English have excluded, and even now exclude the Welsh people from the civilisation of their English neighbours. An Eisteddfod is one of the most mischievous and selfish pieces of sentimentalism which could possibly be perpetrated.' A leading Welsh poet protested; so, six days later, the attack was resumed. 'If it is desirable that the Welsh should talk English, it is monstrous folly to encourage them in a loving fondness for their old language. Not only the energy and power, but the intelligence and music of Europe have come mainly from Teutonic sources, and this glorification of everything Celtic, if it were not pedantry, would be sheer ignorance. The sooner all Welsh specialities disappear from the face of the earth the better.' As for Arnold, he was a sentimentalist who wrote 'arrant nonsense' and 'whose dainty taste requires something more flimsy than the strong sense and sturdy morality of his fellow Englishmen'.

The crude, hot, and barbarous self-righteousness of this was only too typical of English journalism at that time. Hence Arnold's frequent scathing asides on the press. In the present instance, his dislike of intolerance and his belief that the Celtic tradition fostered human values which were under-developed in his brother Saxons provided additional motivation for one of his most equable and most deadly retorts. Having quoted the observations of *The Times*, he continues, 'I am unhappily inured to having these harsh interpretations put by my fellow Englishmen upon what I write, and I no longer cry out about it. And then, too, I have made a study of the Corinthian or leading article style, and know its exigencies, and that they are no more to be quarrelled with than the law of gravitation. So, for my part, when I read these asperities of the *Times*, my mind did not dwell very much on my own concern in them; but what I said to myself, as I put the newspaper down, was this: *"Behold England's difficulty in governing Ireland!"* '

Arnold evidently hoped that his disinterested examination of Celtic culture would contribute in the long run to the reconciliation of England and Ireland by inducing the English to make themselves less Philistine and therefore more agreeable. He hoped for a second result, too.

At the end of his last lecture, he urged the foundation at Oxford of a Professorship of Celtic. Such an act would itself, he said, be 'a message of peace to Ireland'. After a short pause when the lecture was over, the old Principal of Jesus College was heard to say, 'The Angel ended . . .' This tribute, coming from the head of a traditionally Welsh college, must have gratified Arnold quite as much as the more tangible gift which he received in the following year after his concluding lecture as Professor of Poetry. On that occasion, a lady admirer presented him with a keg of whisky.

II

Most of the prose works discussed so far deal ostensibly with literature. Their titles refer to such topics as Homer, Heine, the literary influence of academies, and Celtic literature. But in all of them social criticism is important, too. They direct our attention to what Arnold thought the weaknesses of the English: their intellectual eccentricity and arbitrariness, their self-satisfied Philistinism, their provinciality, and their insensitiveness.

Even to his contemporaries, there was no mistaking the direction in which Arnold's interests were running. The social criticism which he published during the latter half of the eighteen-sixties was the natural outcome of his earlier literary criticism and was closely linked with the educational criticism which was engaging him throughout the decade. His poem 'Obermann Once More', in which he announces his complete emergence from his *Werther* period, expresses the optimistic purposiveness which was his by 1865–6; and it points ahead, beyond his social criticism, to the religious writings which were to occupy him during most of the eighteen-seventies.

(i)

When, in the brief 'Preface' to *Essays in Criticism*, Arnold had good-humouredly ridiculed Fitzjames Stephen's patriotic defence of the British Philistines, he had promised a fuller reply to Stephen and other opponents later. This came early in 1866, when he published an essay, 'My Countrymen', in the *Cornhill Magazine*.

He speaks here with mock humility. He pretends to be cast down by the rebukes administered to him for indecently calling his countrymen Philistines. He has, he says, anxiously discussed the subject with various foreign acquaintances during his recent visit to the Continent and has been grieved to find that they unite in denying intelligence to the great middle class which dominates England now that the era of the aristocracy is over. To the unintelligence of its prepotent bourgeoisie his acquaintances ascribe the country's blundering and capricious foreign policy and its conspicuous failure to solve what they call 'the modern problem'. Their speeches give trenchant expression to convictions which were in fact held by Arnold himself but which he ironically opposes; it is clear that he now locates the head-quarters of Goliath not merely in England but precisely in its middle class.

'What is the modern problem? to make human life, the life of society, all through, more natural and rational; to have the greatest possible number of one's nation happy.' But the condition of the English working class, say the 'envious, carping foreigners', is 'further removed

from civilised and humane life' than that of the working
class 'almost anywhere'. What, then, of the middle
class?

> The fineness and capacity of a man's spirit is shown by his
> enjoyments; your middle class has an enjoyment in its busi-
> ness, we admit, and gets on well in business, and makes
> money; but beyond that? Drugged with business, your
> middle class seems to have its sense blunted for any stimulus
> besides, except religion; it has a religion, narrow, unintelli-
> gent, repulsive. All sincere religion does something for the
> spirit, raises a man out of the bondage of his merely bestial
> part, and saves him; but the religion of your middle class is
> the very lowest form of intelligential life which one can
> imagine as saving. What other enjoyments have they? The
> newspapers, a sort of eating and drinking which are not to
> our taste, a literature of books almost entirely religious or
> semi-religious, books utterly unreadable by an educated
> class anywhere, but which your middle class consumes, they
> say, by the hundred thousand; and in their evenings, for a
> great treat, a lecture on teetotalism or nunneries. Can any
> life be imagined more hideous, more dismal, more unenvi-
> able? Compare it with the life of our middle class as you
> have seen it on the Rhine this summer, or at Lausanne, or
> Zurich. The world of enjoyment, so liberalising and civili-
> sing, belongs to the middle classes there, as well as the world
> of business; the whole world is theirs, they possess life; in
> England the highest class seems to have the monopoly of the
> world of enjoyment, the middle class enjoys itself, as your
> Shakespeare would say, in hugger-mugger, and possesses
> life only by reading in the newspapers, which it does
> devoutly, the doings of great people.

The extravagant flattery of this class by journalists and
politicians can only tend to confirm it in its crudity;
'the civilisation of her middle class is England's capital,
pressing want'.

There was malice in Arnold's choice of a group of
foreigners to utter this criticism of the insular and complacent Philistines. In the *Saturday Review*, Fitzjames
Stephen reacted exactly as might have been expected.
To him, Arnold's friends are 'a gang of foreign Balaams'.
An Englishman enjoys a freedom and wields a power
which they may well envy. It is better to toil in England,
no matter how roughly, coarsely, and meanly, than to
enjoy even 'the most aesthetic form of dawdling that
could be invented by a joint committee from all the
cafés and theatres between the Mediterranean and the
Baltic.'

Stephen's indignation probably encouraged Arnold to
go on criticizing his fellow-countrymen from behind a
penetrable foreign disguise. In two series of letters which
he contributed to the *Pall Mall Gazette* in 1866–7 and
1869–70, the ostensible critic is Arminius von Thunder-
ten-Tronckh, an arrogant young Prussian, the grandson
of the baron in Voltaire's *Candide*. Arnold represents
himself as subdued, a miserable denizen of Grub Street,
feebly striving to defend English life and institutions
against his overbearing and hypercritical friend.

This friend repeatedly denounces the middle class for
believing only in industry and individualism, in 'getting
rich and not being meddled with'. Arnold ineffectually
stands up for it and for its unlovely representative, Bottles,
the manufacturer. On one occasion, Arminius asks what
made Bottles a magistrate. 'His English energy and self-
reliance,' boasts Arnold, 'those same incomparable and
truly British qualities which have just triumphed over
every obstacle and given us the Atlantic telegraph!'
'Pshaw!' retorts Arminius; 'that great rope, with a
Philistine at each end of it talking inutilities!' When
Arminius identifies a living politician, notorious for his

glorification of the middle class, as a descendant of Voltaire's ludicrous optimistic philosopher Pangloss, Arnold gravely suggests that the kinship is not 'in the flesh' but only 'in the spirit'. Again and again his defence serves only to open a way for the Prussian's attack.

Arminius' reiterated advice to the English is that they should get 'Geist' or intelligence. He sneers both at 'the grand, old, fortifying, classical curriculum' which has done so little to give intelligence to Lord Lumpington and at the quackery of the allegedly modern education which has left Bottles entirely raw and unformed. The stupidity of Bottles is even more dangerous than that of the aristocrat; for his is the social class now in power. The members of this class are untouched by the modern spirit and unaware of the modern problem; as a result, England has lately cut a merely ludicrous figure in foreign affairs and is in no very satisfactory condition internally.

At the end of 1870, Arnold allowed Arminius to be killed while serving in the Prussian army against France; and in 1871 he published both series of letters, together with the article 'My Countrymen', as *Friendship's Garland*. The binding was in the spirit of the text: white, or for some copies lavender, cloth, stamped with a mourning band, and with a gilt wreath impressed on the front cover. Despite some archness, *Friendship's Garland* is an entertaining work. It gives amusing expression to some of the leading ideas of *Culture and Anarchy*, applying them especially to questions of foreign policy; and the sixth and seventh letters, which tell how Arminius and Arnold called at the premises where Lord Lumpington and his colleagues were dispensing justice, testify to their author's gift for lively comedy.

(ii)

'Culture and its Enemies', Arnold's last lecture as
Professor of Poetry, was printed in the *Cornhill Magazine*
in 1867. He followed it up in 1868 with five more
articles under the title 'Anarchy and Authority'. After
revision, he issued the whole series as a single volume,
Culture and Anarchy, in January 1869.

These dates are important. Arnold was writing *Culture
and Anarchy* at a time of considerable social and political
unrest. The defeat of Gladstone's Reform Bill in 1866
gave rise to a determined agitation for the extension of
the suffrage. In London, demonstrators invaded Hyde
Park after the police had closed it to them; they tore up
the railings of Park Lane and trampled over the flower-
beds. In Birmingham, Manchester, Glasgow, Leeds,
and elsewhere, mass meetings assembled to hear the
radical John Bright. It soon became clear that the demand
for reform was irresistible; and in 1867 Disraeli introduced, and Parliament passed, a bill which went further
than that defeated in the previous year. This bill enfran-
chised the working men in the towns and almost doubled
the electorate. To many, it seemed a hazardous experi-
ment. Carlyle went so far as to appeal to the aristocracy
to seize power by a *coup d'état*.

Nor were these the only causes for anxiety. The year
1867 saw disturbances among trade unionists, acts of
violence by Fenians, and a series of riots provoked by an
inflammatory anti-Catholic orator named Murphy. It
seemed to many observers, Arnold included, that the
authorities were irresolute and infirm. It was widely
believed that the Home Secretary had shed tears when
harassed by a Reform League deputation. The belief

was groundless. But it was certainly true that the venerable alderman commanding the Royal London Militia had refrained from ordering his men to check certain acts of rowdyism lest the hooligans should turn on them and steal their rifles.

Arnold was level-headed enough to realize that even in these circumstances social chaos was not quite imminent. As an exponent of the modern spirit, moreover, he was in general sympathy with the democratic movement. But he did believe that without order there could be no society; and that there were tendencies in the national life which could, if uncorrected, lead to anarchy. He wrote *Culture and Anarchy* with these very much in mind. Opportunely enough, its last chapter appeared shortly before the first general election under the extended franchise; and the book as a whole came out immediately before the reformed Parliament began work.

The anarchy to which Arnold's title refers is not only social and political but also, fundamentally, intellectual and spiritual. As a remedy, he prescribes culture. 'I am a Liberal,' he states in the 'Introduction', 'yet I am a Liberal tempered by experience, reflection, and renouncement, and I am, above all, a believer in culture.' In what follows, it turns out that 'culture' is not very different from the 'criticism' of his previous writings.

His first chapter, 'Sweetness and Light', defines the good life to which culture directs us. This is characterized by a general harmonious expansion of all our distinctively human powers. Culture teaches a man both to lead such a life himself and to help others to lead it. In saying that religion has an important contribution to make to the fulfilment of this essentially humanistic ideal, Arnold is evidently subordinating religion to culture. He was immediately so understood by the philosopher

Henry Sidgwick, who, censuring 'Culture and its Enemies' as 'ambitious, vague, and perverse', remarks that its author extends to religion a 'languid patronage'.

A full and harmonious self-development being the true object of human endeavour, the other things which men pursue are valuable only in so far as they promote it. They are valuable as means to this end, not as ends in themselves. They are valuable, to use Arnold's term, as 'machinery'. The besetting weakness of the Philistines is, he thinks, their absolute faith in such machinery as freedom, coal, railways, wealth, a growing population, physical health and vigour, and even particular forms of religious organization. Above all, their attachment to these last has severely narrowed their lives. 'Look at the life imaged in such a newspaper as the *Nonconformist*, —a life of jealousy of the Establishment, disputes, tea-meetings, openings of chapels, sermons; and then think of it as an ideal of a human life completing itself on all sides, and aspiring with all its organs after sweetness, light, and perfection!' This was deserved. Victorian Nonconformity could be indescribably dismal, stuffy, and disputatious. At the same time, Arnold's supercilious disdain for it is such that with part of us we welcome Sidgwick's gibe that he appears 'to judge of religious organisations as a dog judges of human beings, chiefly by the scent'.

While Arnold was writing, a new class was gaining a share of political power. He hopes that this, the working class, will not allow itself to be infected by the middle-class worship of machinery; and that such 'Jacobins' as Frederic Harrison will not succeed in converting it to their own fanatical worship of an abstract system of renovation. 'Culture is always assigning to system-makers and systems a smaller share in the bent of human

destiny than their friends like.' What the working class
really needs in view of its new political rôle is the greater
regard for beauty and intelligence, for 'sweetness and
light', which culture gives.

This is the argument of that chapter of *Culture and
Anarchy* which had been Arnold's last lecture as Professor
of Poetry. In addition to Sidgwick, Frederic Harrison
replied to it. In 'Culture: A Dialogue', he pretends to
speak up for the lecture against the strictures of Arnold's
own friend Arminius. Arnold was vastly amused by his
manœuvre. Incoherence and unctuousness are Arminius'
main charges; and it must be granted that there is some
justification for each. Neither this first chapter nor
Culture and Anarchy as a whole is very closely argued; and
Arnold's key notions and phrases, didactically reiterated
in a rather mannered way, can become irritating. But
the easy, lucid, and elegant style of the work, its
sprightly comedy, and its keen and accurate perceptions
make it indisputably a masterpiece of social criticism.

The second chapter condemns as a principle of anarchy
the prevalent English notion 'that it is a most happy and
important thing for a man merely to be able to do as
he likes'. For lately the Englishman has begun to assert
and put in practice 'his right to march where he likes,
meet where he likes, enter where he likes, hoot as he
likes, threaten as he likes, smash as he likes'. Nor do
the authorities try to restrain him. The Alderman-
Colonel's fear for his men and their rifles is notorious.
The Home Secretary states that Murphy showers on the
Catholics language 'only fit to be addressed to thieves or
murderers' but is unwilling to deny Murphy his right of
exercising his liberty. Only against the militant Irish
nationalists, the Fenians, can the authorities act resolutely.
Arnold accounts for this exceptional ability in a passage of

L

brilliantly sustained irony, culminating in a disconcerting
reference to a hideous building in Trafalgar Square.

> In the first place, it never was any part of our creed that the
> great right and blessedness of an Irishman, or, indeed, of
> anybody on earth except an Englishman, is to do as he likes;
> and we can have no scruple at all about abridging, if neces-
> sary, a non-Englishman's assertion of personal liberty. The
> British Constitution, its checks, and its prime virtues, are
> for Englishmen. We may extend them to others out of love
> and kindness; but we find no real divine law written on our
> hearts constraining us so to extend them. And then the
> difference between an Irish Fenian and an English rough is
> so immense, and the case, in dealing with the Fenian, so
> much more clear! He is so evidently desperate and danger-
> ous, a man of a conquered race, a Papist, with centuries of
> ill-usage to inflame him against us, with an alien religion
> established in his country by us at his expense, with no
> admiration of our institutions, no love of our virtues, no
> talents for our business, no turn for our comfort! Show
> him our symbolical Truss Manufactory on the finest site in
> Europe, and tell him that British industrialism and indivi-
> dualism can bring a man to that, and he remains cold!
> Evidently, if we deal tenderly with a sentimentalist like this,
> it is out of pure philanthropy.

What we need, says Arnold, if our individualism is
not to sweep us into anarchy, is 'the notion, so familiar
on the Continent and to antiquity, of *the State*,—the
nation in its collective and corporate character, entrusted
with stringent powers for the general advantage, and con-
trolling individual wills in the name of an interest wider
than that of individuals'. But to whom can we entrust
this authority? The aristocracy is impervious to ideas;
the middle class is narrow and self-satisfied; the working
class is rude and intemperate. None of them is fit to
take control. The only solution is for members of all of

them, with the help of culture, to outgrow their ordinary class limitations, to apprehend the principles by which a just exercise of state power would be regulated, and to make the state in this way an expression of their 'best self'.

It is obvious that Arnold, in saying this, does not suppose that he is bringing forward a complete scheme for the immediate establishment of 'a firm State-power'. He is appealing rather for a change of attitude towards public authority on the part of private citizens—a change such as has very largely taken place in this country since he wrote. Such a change will, he feels, enable the state to act firmly and decisively when necessary—perhaps to organize secondary education, perhaps even to gag Murphy.

Further thoughts on the three main social classes open the next chapter. Arnold epitomizes these in the three nicknames listed in its title, 'Barbarians, Philistines, Populace'. Still developing views already expressed, he declares that the firm state-power for which he looks will be acceptable only in so far as it is seen to operate not on behalf of this or that class but on behalf of the 'best self' or essential *humanity* of all citizens. But how favourable is the contemporary environment to the belief that there exists any such ground for the erection of an impartial public authority?

In answering this question, Arnold produces some of his most spirited satire. The faith of the English in doing as one likes makes them unwilling to recognize a 'best self', a 'paramount authority', in literature or religion or politics. Arnold illustrates this unwillingness by telling, among other things, how a Nonconformist friend of his once countered a harsh comment in the *Saturday Review* on a favourite lecturer by placidly quoting the narrowly partisan *British Banner* in the lecturer's favour. 'The speaker had evidently no notion that there was a scale of value for judgments on these topics, and that the judgments of the *Saturday Review* ranked high on this scale, and those of the *British Banner* low; the taste of the bathos implanted by nature in the literary judgments of man had never, in my friend's case, encountered any let or hindrance.'

The environment, then, is unhelpful; indeed, it is obstructive. The newspapers are especially culpable. Some of them sow an entire disbelief in 'a best self and a right reason having claim to paramount authority'; others disseminate the *laissez-faire* theory that right reason will providentially emerge if each of us continues to act on the promptings of his ordinary self. How necessary it is that there should be 'some public recognition and establishment of our best self, or right reason'.

There will be nothing of the kind while we continue in all circumstances to prefer doing to thinking, to pride ourselves on our energy at the expense of our intelligence. For there are two forces which regulate human life. Following Heine, Arnold names these Hebraism and Hellenism. The one mobilizes our moral impulses, the other our intellectual impulses; the one promotes activity, the other understanding. In general, Hebraism is the more important of the two.

Since the Renaissance, however, the main stream of man's advance has been in the direction indicated by Hellenism. The modern spirit is a critical spirit, seeking and diffusing sweetness and light. But Puritanism, a tyrannical form of Hebraism, has prevented the English from recognizing this fact. A result is the 'confusion and false movement' already analysed.

This discussion of Hebraism and Hellenism occupies

the fourth chapter; in the fifth, Arnold warns his fellow-countrymen in more detail of the danger to which their fanatical Hebraism exposes them.

> The Puritan's great danger is that he imagines himself in possession of a rule telling him the *unum necessarium*, or one thing needful, and that he then remains satisfied with a very crude conception of what this rule really is and what it tells him, thinks he has now knowledge and henceforth needs only to act, and, in this dangerous state of assurance and self-satisfaction, proceeds to give full swing to a number of the instincts of his ordinary self. Some of the instincts of his ordinary self he has, by the help of his rule of life, conquered; but others which he has not conquered by this help he is so far from perceiving to need subjugation, and to be instincts of an inferior self, that he even fancies it to be his right and duty, in virtue of having conquered a limited part of himself, to give unchecked swing to the remainder. He is, I say, a victim of Hebraism, of the tendency to cultivate strictness of conscience rather than spontaneity of consciousness. And what he wants is a larger conception of human nature, showing him the number of other points at which his nature must come to its best, besides the points which he himself knows and thinks of.

This is a subtle and revealing analysis; and Arnold goes on to show that the Victorian Philistine's narrow-minded concentration upon 'machinery', upon making money and saving his soul, needs to be corrected by an infusion of Hellenism. His conclusion is that 'the development of our Hellenising instincts, seeking ardently the intelligible law of things, and making a stream of fresh thought play freely about our stock notions and habits, is what is most wanted by us at present'.

This completes the main argument of the book. From his preliminary declaration, Arnold has advanced to a fuller discussion of the danger of political anarchy, mainly in his second and third chapters, and to a closer consideration of the underlying drift towards intellectual and spiritual anarchy, mainly in his fourth and fifth chapters. In a final chapter, illustrating the Hellenizing approach to current political questions, he turns 'a stream of fresh thought' upon the stock notions and pieces of mental petrifaction to which his fellow-Liberals appeal in support of their policies.

While discussing one of these policies, free trade, Arnold takes the opportunity of quoting from *The Times* a pompous and smug assurance that, since economic laws are beyond human control, nobody can be held responsible for the slumps which periodically devastate the East End of London. 'There is no one to blame for this; it is the result of Nature's simplest laws!' With a grim irony, Arnold describes this as an 'imposing and colossal necessitarianism'. School-inspection often takes him to the East End; so he has transcribed for himself this specimen of *The Times*' 'firm philosophy', and carries it about with him in order to fortify himself against 'the depressing sights which on these occasions assail' him: for example, 'children eaten up with disease, half-sized, half-fed, half-clothed, neglected by their parents, without health, without home, without hope'. It is regrettable that there is no record of Arnold's having read *Hard Times*. Could his assent to the message of that novel have been less complete than was Ruskin's? or less ready than his own recognition of the two dominant types of British Philistinism in Murdstone and Quinion of *David Copperfield*?

Arnold's last word is that the true business of the friends of culture in Victorian England is 'to get men to try, in preference to staunchly acting with imperfect knowledge, to obtain some sounder basis of knowledge on which to act'. This advice appears also in the 'Preface' which he added when he assembled the essays for publication in book form.

Readers sometimes complain that his terminology in *Culture and Anarchy* is vague. But it would be absurd to try to read the book as a philosophical treatise. Such words as 'culture', 'best self', and 'ordinary self' convey clearly enough the kind of framework of ideas within which Arnold makes his criticism of contemporary life; and it is this criticism that matters. Many circumstances have changed since he wrote. But *Culture and Anarchy* is of enduring interest as the expression of a nimble intuitive intelligence playing freely on the life of an energetic and blundering age; and we have only to recall the personages introduced by Arnold as representatives of that age—Murphy, John Bright, the Alderman-Colonel, and the rest—to be at once reminded that it is also the expression of a resourceful comic talent.

(iii)

The practical lesson of Arnold's social criticism is that culture—disseminated, in part, by organized secondary education—can help the transition to democracy, inevitable in any case, to occur without disaster. In his religious criticism he again assumes the inevitability of a change. The modern spirit, he thinks, has made belief in the supernatural impossible for many Englishmen; before long it will have made it impossible for very many more. The process is painful, and Arnold has no wish to accelerate it. But he is anxious that those whom it overtakes should not discard religion itself under the erroneous impression that it has no foundation other than a belief in the supernatural.

To Arnold, as to his father, religion is essentially
morality; and he holds that the truth of morality can be
confirmed by the only test which will satisfy the modern
spirit, the test of experience. By this, men can satisfy
themselves that happiness is dependent upon righteousness. But religion is not simply morality. What men
will do in obedience to a bare moral precept is slight
compared with what they will do to please God. Religion, in fact, is 'morality touched with emotion'.

The essence of Christianity is the knowledge that men
can so identify themselves with Jesus that they die to
their ordinary selves and rise again in this world to
genuine life. For Arnold, 'resurrection' is not 'life
after death'; he rejects all miracles, including the
Incarnation; and he discards the unverifiable propositions,
such as those concerning the Trinity, which are advanced
by theologians. When the Bible itself seems to advance
such propositions, or to assert the truth of miracles, he
understands its language emotively and not referentially;
he reads it as 'Literature' or poetry and not as 'Dogma'
or science. The furthest that he will go in the direction
of theology is to define God, in terms which got him into
trouble with the philosopher F. H. Bradley, as '*the
enduring power, not ourselves, which makes for righteousness*'.

He believes that a person who holds these views may
be a sincere member of the Anglican church. Indeed,
one of his purposes in trying to demonstrate the irrele-
vance to true religion of most theological dogmas is to
clear away impediments to the union of all Christians
in this body. For the separatism of the dissenters has
condemned them to provinciality. Their entry into a
national church would be greatly to their intellectual and
spiritual advantage. It would also make the Church of
England what Dr. Arnold had wished it to be.

These ideas are expounded in *St. Paul and Protestantism* (1870), *Literature and Dogma* (1873), *God and the Bible* (1875), and *Last Essays on Church and Religion* (1877). They excited great interest, friendly and unfriendly, at the time. Some of the 'vivacities' accompanying their expression gave offence. This was regrettable, and Arnold later erased offending passages, as he had earlier done with *Essays in Criticism*. Even so, the free-thinking of this regular church-goer and Bible-reader remains intolerable to the orthodox. At present, there are signs of a renewed sympathetic interest in the kind of undogmatic religion which he taught. Whether this persists or not, readers of his religious writings may still be charmed by his sincere if not at all points logically defensible attempt to ensure that ideas and practices which he believed important to the human spirit should not be jettisoned along with beliefs incapable of enduring the scientific climate.

Although she did not read his religious books, his wife was very ready to reassure anxious friends. 'Matt', she used to say, 'is a good Christian at bottom.'

III

By this time Arnold had established his main principles as a critic of literature, education, politics, and religion. Their application to particular fresh topics, and especially to literary and political topics, was what mainly engaged him after the completion of the last of his religious books. Four collections contain most of the resulting studies: *Mixed Essays* (1879), *Irish Essays* (1882), *Discourses in America* (1885), and a second, posthumous series of *Essays in Criticism* (1888).

(i)

The first of these opens with an essay, 'Democracy', which had originally served as 'Preface' to his *Popular Education in France* (1861). This is a sober and persuasive formulation of the case for an extension of state power, especially in the field of secondary education. In *Irish Essays*, secondary education is a major preoccupation. At present, says Arnold, the English middle class is 'brought up in the worst and most ignoble secondary schools in Western Europe'. A better training could more completely humanize its members and so make them less obnoxious to the Irish. For Arnold holds that to attach Ireland to England it is necessary not only that the English should '*do* something different from what they have done hitherto' but also that they should '*be* something different from what they have been hitherto'. He had outlined this view twenty years earlier at the end of his *Study of Celtic Literature*.

The only recent literary study included in *Irish Essays*, one illustrating the persistence of Arnold's old love for the theatre, is 'The French Play in London'. It contains another characteristic plea for state intervention, this time to organize the theatre. Aided and guided by the state, this would be better able to exert its civilizing influence.

Civilization still means for Arnold the full and harmonious development of the distinctively human powers of the individuals who compose society. Again and again he lists these powers as 'the power of conduct, the power of intellect and knowledge, the power of beauty, the power of social life and manners'. Of the terms which he had used in *Culture and Anarchy*, Hebraism is equivalent to the first of these, Hellenism comprises the other three.

The English Hebraize too exclusively; but the French do not Hebraize enough. In several of his later essays, and notably in 'Numbers', the first of the *Discourses in America*, Arnold expresses his fear of the consequences to French civilization of the increasing lewdness which he claims to observe in French life. His terms for this, 'Lubricity' and 'Aselgeia', convey an unctuous censoriousness which suggests that on this subject his disinterestedness is far from perfect. There was, in fact, in Arnold a distinct strain of prudishness; even in *Culture and Anarchy* his discussion of Liberal policies seems least disinterested when he comes to deal with the Deceased Wife's Sister Bill.

Nevertheless, Arnold still professes disinterestedness; and on most subjects he does to a remarkable extent achieve it. The critical attitude to which he aspires is admirably described in the first of the *Irish Essays*: 'I imagine myself to be at present talking quietly to open-minded, unprejudiced, simple people, free from class spirit and party spirit, resolved to forswear self-delusion and make-believe, not to be pedants, but to see things as they really are.' A seventeenth-century exponent of this spirit, Lucius Cary, Lord Falkland, is the subject of one of the most attractive of the *Mixed Essays*.

Falkland had been a favourite of Arnold's father. Arnold himself sees him as one who did not remain aloof from action but who was incapable of serving either King or Parliament in any narrowly partisan fashion. He fell at Newbury in 1643. In Arnold's opinion, he and not Hampden was the true martyr of the Civil War. 'He was the martyr of lucidity of mind and largeness of temper, in a strife of imperfect intelligences and tempers illiberal.' To this exemplar of virtues still regrettably rare in the nineteenth century, Arnold devotes one of the most delicate and deeply felt of his biographical sketches.

It is with a genuine disinterestedness such as he ascribes to Falkland that in several of his later essays he discusses the structure of contemporary English society and expresses his mature conviction that 'immense inequalities of condition and property' are an obstacle to civilization. Indeed, social equality is the theme of his most valuable political criticism during this period.

He himself dated his perception of his country's need for greater equality from his first inspectorial mission to the Continent in 1859. He had touched on the subject ten years afterwards while criticizing in *Culture and Anarchy* a Real Estate Intestacy Bill. Ten years later still, he issued the classical statement of his belief, 'Equality', the second of the *Mixed Essays*.

This is a superb performance. Composed for delivery as a lecture to a well-to-do audience, it is an elegant and courteous, but quite unambiguous statement of the damage done to the British by their 'religion of inequality'. Arnold's initial approach to his subject is characteristic of his tactics throughout. He wishes to cite Menander's maxim, 'Choose equality and flee greed', but not to intrude it too provocatively upon his hearers. So he quotes first the irreproachable maxim, 'Evil communications corrupt good manners'. Nothing could be more acceptable; the sentence is sanctioned by its use in the New Testament, in the Burial Service, and even in school copy-books. But it was probably in the first place a line of Menander's. Why, then, should not Arnold take another maxim from so respectable a source? He does so: 'Choose equality and flee greed.'

Despite this cautious procedure, Arnold speaks crisply
and firmly when he arrives at his conclusions:

What the middle class sees is that splendid piece of material-
ism, the aristocratic class, with a wealth and luxury utterly
out of their reach, with a standard of social life and manners,
the offspring of that wealth and luxury, seeming utterly out
of their reach also. And thus they are thrown back upon
themselves,—upon a defective type of religion, a narrow
range of intellect and knowledge, a stunted sense of beauty,
a low standard of manners. And the lower class see before
them the aristocratic class, and its civilisation, such as it is,
even infinitely more out of *their* reach than out of that of the
middle class; while the life of the middle class, with its
unlovely types of religion, thought, beauty, and manners,
has naturally, in general, no great attractions for them either.
And so they too are thrown back upon themselves; upon
their beer, their gin, and their *fun*. Now, then, you will
understand what I meant by saying that our inequality
materialises our upper class, vulgarises our middle class,
brutalises our lower.

Elsewhere, Arnold recognizes that the love of liberty
and the love of equality are alike manifestations of that
instinct of expansion in man which is responsible for the
whole democratic movement. The English have made
something of a fetish of the one; but they have little or
no taste for the other. So certain is Arnold, however, of
the civilizing effect of equality that he is ready to curtail
liberty for its sake. At the end of 'Equality', he recommends interference by the state with a testator's freedom
to dispose of the whole of his own property. To
twentieth-century readers, such a proposal will seem
moderate enough. But it is not Arnold's only expression
of dissent from 'the superstitious worship of property';
and at the date at which it was made it testified

unequivocally to the strength and earnestness of its author's concern for social equality.

(ii)

'Whoever seriously occupies himself with literature, will soon perceive its vital connexion with other agencies. Suppose a man to be ever so much convinced that literature is, as indisputably it is, a powerful agency for benefiting the world and for civilising it, such a man cannot but see that there are many obstacles preventing what is salutary in literature from gaining general admission, and from producing due effect.' In these words from the 'Preface' to *Mixed Essays*, Arnold alludes to the considerations which had led him for a time to forsake literary for social and religious criticism. After 1877, these considerations still led him, as we have seen, to urge social equality, secondary education, and the rest upon the triumphant Philistines; but they did not then prevent him from adding considerably to his strictly literary criticism.

In this literary criticism of his last years, he is more directly concerned with English poetry than ever before. The central document is an essay originally published in 1880 as the 'General Introduction' to T. H. Ward's four-volume anthology *The English Poets* and reprinted as 'The Study of Poetry' in *Essays in Criticism: Second Series*. In this, Arnold begins by recalling his conviction that the dogmatic elements in Christianity are less enduring than the poetic elements. As belief in the former fails, men will come increasingly to rely upon the latter; indeed, they will come increasingly to rely upon poetry in general. 'More and more mankind will discover that we have to turn to poetry to interpret life for us, to console us, to sustain us. Without poetry, our science will appear incomplete; and most of what now passes with us for religion and philosophy will be replaced by poetry.'

In this connection, Arnold describes poetry as 'a criticism of life'. Sixteen years earlier, in an essay on Joseph Joubert, he had applied the same phrase to imaginative literature generally. Disparagers of Arnold—Lytton Strachey, for instance—have leapt at the chance of understanding its key word to suit themselves and so gaining an easy if unreal victory. But there can be no excuse for not knowing what Arnold means by criticism: a disinterested attempt to see things as they are, in the course of which value-judgments naturally and almost insensibly form themselves. What is there unacceptable in this as a description of the ideal attitude of a creative artist towards his experience? Is it not because imaginative literature really is, in Arnold's sense, a criticism of life that Dr. I. A. Richards can speak of it as constituting with the other arts 'our storehouse of recorded values' and Mr. Ezra Pound can suggest that its function may be to 'incite humanity to continue living'?

Only the best poetry is capable of performing the task which Arnold assigns to it. So it is important that readers should learn to choose the best. Arnold warns them against two kinds of fallacious judgment: the historic estimate and the personal estimate. But how are they to arrive at the real estimate?

'Critics', says Arnold, 'give themselves great labour to draw out what in the abstract constitutes the characters of a high quality of poetry. It is much better simply to have recourse to concrete examples;—to take specimens of poetry of the high, the very highest quality, and to say: The characters of a high quality of poetry are what is expressed *there*.' Arnold does precisely this; and he suggests that short passages and single lines such as he quotes from Homer, Dante, Shakespeare, and Milton may be lodged in the memory and applied as touchstones to other poetry. This other poetry must not be required to resemble them; but if the touchstone-quotations are used with tact they will enable readers to detect 'the presence or absence of high poetic quality'. This is essentially the comparative method which Arnold had used from the start and by means of which in the present essay he shows that the *Chanson de Roland* does not merit praise such as men give to the *Iliad* and that Shelley's ardours seem unimportant when confronted by Burns' humanity. But it is regrettable that the touchstone-quotations which he provides, instead of representing as far as possible the full range and variety of poetic excellence, are predominantly of one type. They are passages in what he calls 'the grand style'; and they express above all melancholy and deprivation. Remembering Arnold's own aims and achievements in poetry, one cannot avoid the suspicion that the personal here contaminates the real estimate.

The remainder of the essay consists of a swift review of English poetry from Chaucer to Burns. It is notorious that in it Arnold admits to the ranks of the greatest poets, of the unquestionable 'classics', only Shakespeare and Milton; that he examines Chaucer, Dryden, Pope, and Burns only to exclude them; and that he does not mention Donne. What is less generally realized is how very high he draws the line separating the classics from all other poets and how ready he is to acknowledge the value of the best of those whom he places below this line. In a letter written at the same time as 'The Study of Poetry' he refers to Chaucer and Burns and remarks 'what a glorious set of five these two, with Wordsworth, Milton and Shakespeare, make for our English poetry. If we add Spenser, Gray, and Keats, we shall have a set of eight, and where is it to be matched outside of the Greeks?' Nevertheless, his praise of Chaucer and Burns is too restricted; and he omits Dryden and Pope even from his list of eight.

'The substance of Chaucer's poetry, his view of things and his criticism of life, has largeness, freedom, shrewdness, benignity; but it has not . . . high seriousness.' This quality is missing in Burns, too. Arnold cites Aristotle, always one of his most trusted authorities, in support of his insistence upon it. But, as he speaks, 'high seriousness' comes to seem uncomfortably like 'solemnity'; and our thoughts move back to his touchstone-quotations. A reference, in 'The French Play in London', to 'poetry of the most serious and elevated kind' confirms our suspicions. We conclude that Arnold, in his critical as in his creative writings, was too little able to liberate himself from the nineteenth-century fixation upon 'elevated' poetry.

If his bondage to it impairs his appreciation of Chaucer and Burns, it incapacitates him as a critic of Dryden and Pope. As usual, he moves with circumspection. 'I cast about for some mode of arriving . . . at . . . [the real] estimate without offence. And perhaps the best way is to begin, as it is easy to begin, with cordial praise.' He praises 'Dryden as the puissant and glorious founder, Pope as the splendid high priest, of our age of prose and reason'. But he cannot agree that theirs is the verse of 'men whose criticism of life has a high seriousness, or even, without that high seriousness, has poetic largeness, freedom, insight, benignity'. In short, they 'are not classics of our poetry, they are classics of our prose'.

M

Our most important poet of their period is Gray; and his work is slighter and less perfect than it might have been had he lived in a more congenial age.

Later in the same volume, in 'Thomas Gray', Arnold amplifies this view. But the best-known statement in this essay refers to Dryden and Pope. 'The difference between genuine poetry and the poetry of Dryden, Pope, and all their school, is briefly this: their poetry is conceived and composed in their wits, genuine poetry is conceived and composed in the soul.' In these words Arnold reaffirms his previous estimate of Dryden and Pope and again exposes the preconceptions regarding poetry which sustain it. Thanks to these, he is prompt to appreciate loftiness and energy; but he has relatively little taste for colloquialism and complexity. His ignoring of Donne calls for no further explanation—though in justice it should be mentioned that his letters contain favourable allusions to other 'metaphysicals'.

Despite recurrent references to *King Lear* as one of the supreme works of the creative imagination, Arnold nowhere writes at length on Shakespeare. But he gives two essays to Milton, the other of 'our poetical classics'. The more interesting of these is 'A French Critic on Milton' in *Mixed Essays*. Arnold here comments upon a recent French study of Milton, comparing it with those of Macaulay, Addison, and Johnson, in such a way as to record his own view of Milton more fully than anywhere else. The subject of *Paradise Lost* displeases him: it is a story, intended to be taken literally, 'which many of even the most religious people nowadays hesitate to take literally; while yet, upon our being able to take it literally, the whole real interest of the poem for us depends. Merely as matter of poetry, the story of the Fall has no special force or effectiveness; its effectiveness for us comes, and can only come, from our taking it all as the literal narrative of what positively happened.' Nevertheless, Milton is a classic: 'he is our great artist in style, our one first-rate master in the grand style'. In *Essays in Criticism: Second Series*, Arnold suggests in a short address on Milton that this style by its nobility may help to refine and elevate the Anglo-Saxon Philistines on both sides of the Atlantic.

Most of the remaining essays in this collection are devoted to the poets of the earlier part of Arnold's own century. He had already attempted in 'Heinrich Heine' and in 'The Function of Criticism at the Present Time' to revalue these poets for his own generation, for one, that is, in partial reaction against Romanticism. In these late essays, he reconsiders four of them separately.

He believes Keats 'to have been by his promise, at any rate, if not fully by his performance, one of the very greatest of English poets'. This conviction is founded not only upon the poetry but also upon a knowledge of its author. Keats was not the sensuous weakling he is sometimes supposed to have been. There was 'flint and iron in him'. Had he been granted more time, he would assuredly have developed greatly; and, in the terms used in Arnold's study of Celtic literature, he would as a poet have added 'moral profundity' to his 'natural magic'. As it is, in natural magic he ranks with Shakespeare.

This line of argument produces a mainly biographical essay; the study of Shelley, occasioned by Edward Dowden's life of the poet, is almost wholly biographical. In each, Arnold writes of the sexual life of his subject with the prudish censoriousness already noticed. So marked is his distaste for Shelley's 'inflammability' that even a final recapitulation of his virtues fails to restore

M*

the balance. Perceiving this, he planned to write something more on the subject, but he was prevented by
death.

His description of Shelley the poet is famous: a 'beautiful and ineffectual angel, beating in the void his luminous
wings in vain'. To much the same effect, though less
lyrically, Tennyson in later life once quoted a passage
by Shelley and said, 'There he seems to me to go up in
the air and burst'. Arnold prefers Byron. Byron and
Wordsworth, by their actual performance and despite
the likelihood that Keats possessed a richer natural en-
dowment than either of them, are the pre-eminent
English poets of their century. Byron's value is of the
same kind as Heine's; it springs from his having thrown
himself into a desperate battle with Philistinism. He was
a 'passionate and dauntless soldier of a forlorn hope, who,
ignorant of the future and unconsoled by its promises,
nevertheless waged against the conservation of the old
impossible world so fiery battle; waged it till he fell,—
waged it with such splendid and imperishable excellence
of sincerity and strength.'

But Wordsworth is his superior. In fact, the only
moderns who certainly excel Wordsworth are Dante,
Shakespeare, Molière, Milton, and Goethe. His work
has moral profundity. 'A large sense is of course to be
given to the term *moral*. Whatever bears upon the
question, "how to live," comes under it.' Arnold,
having occupied this position, attacks the current doctrine of art for art's sake. 'A poetry of revolt against
moral ideas is a poetry of revolt against *life*; a poetry of
indifference towards moral ideas is a poetry of indifference towards *life*.' It is not surprising that this passage
should be one of those into which Arnold introduces his
description of poetry as a criticism of life. The context

elucidates the phrase and supports the interpretation already given.

Having claimed that Wordsworth's poetry has moral profundity, Arnold at once denies that it embodies a valuable 'philosophy'. It is difficult to see how it can have the one without embodying at least something of the other, if only in embryonic form. But the over-emphasis was perhaps necessary if Arnold was to achieve his laudable aim of deflecting attention from Words-worth's more abstract moralizings to his more genuinely creative works.

In what, then, resides the superiority of Wordsworth to all those poets whom Arnold has subordinated to him? The answer to this question completes the argument of the essay on Wordsworth; and it is conveniently sum-marized in the essay on Byron. 'It is in the power with which Wordsworth feels the resources of joy offered to us in nature, offered to us in the primary human affec-tions and duties, and in the power with which, in his moments of inspiration, he renders this joy, and makes us, too, feel it; a force greater than himself seeming to lift him and to prompt his tongue, so that he speaks in a style far above any style of which he has the constant command, and with a truth far beyond any philosophic truth of which he has the conscious and assured posses-sion.'

IV

It is unfortunate that Arnold's appreciation of the artistic potentialities of the novel should have remained relatively undeveloped. Admittedly, his poem 'Haworth Churchyard' contains one of the earliest tributes to the power of *Wuthering Heights*; he has essays on George

Sand and Tolstoy, in the latter of which he contrasts the
Russian's treatment of Anna Karenina with Flaubert's
hounding down of Emma Bovary; he makes references in
this and other essays to various English novelists; and it
would seem from his note-books that during his last
years novels were securing an increased, though still
small, share of his reading-time. But this hardly amounts
to a sustained, serious interest in his own age's main
form of literary expression; and nowhere does he utter
an opinion on the work of that novelist whom more than
any other he was fitted sympathetically to understand,
George Eliot.

In so far as he is a strictly literary critic, he is mainly
a critic of poetry; and his rank must be determined by
such things as his lectures *On Translating Homer* and his
essays 'Heinrich Heine', 'Wordsworth', 'Byron', and
'The Study of Poetry'. Even here, however, his admiration for the grand style causes him, as I have already
remarked, to undervalue colloquialism and complexity.
Nor is this his only conspicuous limitation. Despite his
admiration for French civilization, he is notably unap-
preciative of French poetry. Comparing France's 'established national metre for high poetry', the rhymed
alexandrine, with English blank verse, he insists, in
'Maurice de Guérin' and again in 'The French Play in
London', that it is, like the heroic couplet of eighteenth-
century England, 'a form radically inadequate and
inferior'.

Readers occasionally allege a more general disability,
namely, that he tries to measure poetry by an arbitrary
external standard. Those who dread some such dicta-
torial design will naturally find utterances upon which to
feed their apprehensions. But to do so is to forget
Arnold's steady insistence that criticism is essentially the

exercise of curiosity and that the really valuable judgment forms itself almost insensibly in the course of an attempt 'to see the object as in itself it really is'.

What literary judgment is concerned with is the object's power of satisfying, in the words of the 1853 'Preface', 'the great primary human affections: . . . those elementary feelings which subsist permanently in the race, and which are independent of time'. When Arnold recommends the use of touchstone-quotations, he is simply suggesting that readers can, by reminding themselves of poetry which has moved them at this level in the past, help themselves to a more secure judgment of that which actually confronts them. Towards the end of his *Practical Criticism* Dr. I. A. Richards describes a technique for ascertaining whether the feelings excited by a poem do or do not 'come from a deep source in our experience'. Arnold recommends touchstone-quotations for precisely this purpose. Is it not likely that most readers would find the use of these simpler, more natural, and more effective than Dr. Richards' formal drill?

Distinguished as is Arnold's achievement in the best of his criticism of particular works and particular authors, it is probably less important than his achievement as a spokesman for criticism itself, as a champion of literary culture. 'The Function of Criticism at the Present Time' is both the classical apologia for the rôle which Arnold himself sustained with such effect and the classical statement of the liberal principles which ideally should guide its performance. 'The Literary Influence of Academies' is a persuasive reminder of the authority of standards of criticism. A general disregard for these would produce consequences which would not be confined to literature; and there was much in Arnold's

environment, as there is in ours, to discourage any regard
for them. So in *Culture and Anarchy* Arnold turns his
attention to this environment and produces the wisest
and wittiest of his longer prose works. His lively comic
sense, wide acquaintance with English life, quick perceptions, alert intelligence, and fundamental seriousness
are all evident here. Compared with these works in
which he draws so extensively on his powers and experience, Arnold's poetry appears narrow in theme and
monotonous in tone and feeling. To say so much is not,
of course, to deny its sincerity and charm; nor is it to
forget its occasional extraordinary power.

In his various prose writings, it is above all Arnold's
sanity, his clear sense of things as they are, which is
impressive. None of the other Victorian prophets with
whom he is sometimes bracketed can claim this quality
in anything like the same degree. Beside him, Carlyle
looks grotesquely prejudiced, Ruskin febrile and unbal-
anced, Morris irresponsibly escapist. Even Mill, despite
the saintliness of his rationalism, looks like the victim of
a system.

To Arnold, a system was merely a mechanism for
falsifying one's perceptions. In Frederic Harrison's
'Culture: A Dialogue', Arminius blames Arnold for
lacking a philosophy with 'coherent[,] . . . interdepen-
dent, subordinate, and derivative' principles. Arnold
saw his opportunity; the accusation was a perfect target
for his ridicule, and he kept it under steady and shattering
fire. In 'A French Critic on Goethe', he describes sys-
tematic literary criticism, by which he means criticism
which pronounces judgment not in accordance with what
it finds in the text but in accordance with some external
system of beliefs, as 'the most worthless of all'.

Without relying upon any such external system for

support, Arnold speaks with a quiet confidence in the justness of his particular perceptions. As we have seen, he is hard to please; but even his dissatisfaction with a book or institution or dogma usually finds delicate and urbane expression. So much so that a contemporary rightly credited him with having helped appreciably 'to raise our standard of criticism above that of the old slashing, rough-and-ready clubmen of literature'.

At the same time, it must be admitted that he can seem distinctly supercilious. Hearing of his death, an acquaintance was moved to exclaim, 'Poor Arnold! he won't like God'. A lifelong friend gives an excellent description of the effect of his polite, aloof raillery in controversy. 'It cannot be denied that he had the art, when he chose to use it, of making those whom he criticized look supremely ridiculous, and people put into such a position do not always see the fun of it so clearly as others. Nay, they are apt sometimes to get very angry, and to curse and swear (in a literary sense) so as to lay themselves open to fresh castigation from their amused tormentor. All the more if the punishment is bestowed with imperturbable good humour, with serene superiority and with an air of innocence and wonder very funny but very exasperating.' So important was controversy in Arnold's literary life that no account of his criticism could be complete without the introduction of such opponents as F. W. Newman and Fitzjames Stephen.

Arnold's self-assurance did not impair his fair-mindedness. He strove to achieve a full view of things even in circumstances in which it might have seemed that a partial view would provide a more effective basis for prompt and vigorous action. I have already quoted examples of those returns upon himself which testify so clearly to his flexibility, his moderation, and his 'justness of spirit'; and these are qualities which may be felt throughout his work.

Sane, confident, urbane, and fair-minded; experienced and perceptive; free from any compulsion to crush his notions into a system—Arnold is indubitably the central man of letters of his age. Its most distinguished poet is the author of the words which I should like to set down in conclusion. Replying to a friend who evidently disliked Arnold's tone, G. M. Hopkins says: 'I do not like your calling Matthew Arnold Mr. Kidglove Cocksure. I have more reason than you for disagreeing with him and thinking him very wrong, but nevertheless I am sure he is a rare genius and a great critic.'

SELECT BIBLIOGRAPHY

1. Arnold's Chief Works, in Order of Publication

THE STRAYED REVELLER, AND OTHER POEMS (Fellowes, 1849).

EMPEDOCLES ON ETNA, AND OTHER POEMS (Fellowes, 1852).

POEMS (Longmans, 1853).

POEMS: SECOND SERIES (Longmans, 1855).

MEROPE (Longmans, 1858).

POPULAR EDUCATION IN FRANCE (Longmans, 1861).

ON TRANSLATING HOMER (Longmans, 1861).

LAST WORDS ON TRANSLATING HOMER (Longmans, 1862).

A FRENCH ETON (Macmillan, 1864).

ESSAYS IN CRITICISM [First Series] (Macmillan, 1865).

ON THE STUDY OF CELTIC LITERATURE (Smith, Elder, 1867).

NEW POEMS (Macmillan, 1867).

SCHOOLS AND UNIVERSITIES ON THE CONTINENT (Macmillan, 1868).

CULTURE AND ANARCHY (Smith, Elder, 1869).

ST. PAUL AND PROTESTANTISM (Smith, Elder, 1870).

FRIENDSHIP'S GARLAND (Smith, Elder, 1871).

LITERATURE AND DOGMA (Smith, Elder, 1873).

GOD AND THE BIBLE (Smith, Elder, 1875).

LAST ESSAYS ON CHURCH AND RELIGION (Smith, Elder, 1877).

MIXED ESSAYS (Smith, Elder, 1879).

IRISH ESSAYS AND OTHERS (Smith, Elder, 1882).

DISCOURSES IN AMERICA (Macmillan, 1885).

ESSAYS IN CRITICISM: SECOND SERIES (Macmillan, 1888).

REPORTS ON ELEMENTARY SCHOOLS, 1852–1882, edited by Sir F. Sandford (Macmillan, 1889).

LETTERS OF MATTHEW ARNOLD, 1848–1888, 2 vols., edited by G. W. E. Russell (Macmillan, 1895).

UNPUBLISHED LETTERS OF MATTHEW ARNOLD, edited by A. Whitridge (Yale University Press, 1923).

THE LETTERS OF MATTHEW ARNOLD TO ARTHUR HUGH CLOUGH, edited by H. F. Lowry (Oxford University Press, 1932).

THE NOTE-BOOKS OF MATTHEW ARNOLD, edited by H. F. Lowry, K. Young, and W. H. Dunn (Oxford University Press, 1952).

This list may be supplemented by reference to T. B. Smart, THE BIBLIOGRAPHY OF MATTHEW ARNOLD (Davy, 1892).

2. *Some Modern Editions and Reprints*

POETICAL WORKS, edited by C. B. Tinker and H. F. Lowry, (Oxford University Press, 1950).

EMPÉDOCLE SUR L'ETNA, edited by Louis Bonnerot (Aubier, Paris, 1947).

CULTURE AND ANARCHY, edited by J. Dover Wilson (Cambridge University Press, 1932).

The first series of ESSAYS IN CRITICISM and the Homer lectures are printed together as ESSAYS LITERARY AND CRITICAL in Everyman's Library (Dent); ESSAYS IN CRITICISM: SECOND SERIES is included in the Scholar's Library (Macmillan).

MATTHEW ARNOLD: POETRY AND PROSE, edited by John Bryson (Hart-Davis, 1954). A comprehensive general selection.

The standard collected edition is THE WORKS OF MATTHEW ARNOLD, 15 vols. (Macmillan, 1903–4). This is very scarce.

3. *Some Biographical and Critical Works*

MATTHEW ARNOLD, POÈTE, by Louis Bonnerot (Didier, Paris, 1947). A searching study of the poems as material for a psychological biography of the poet.

MATTHEW ARNOLD: A STUDY IN CONFLICT, by E. K. Brown (Chicago University Press, 1948).

MATTHEW ARNOLD, by E. K. Chambers (Oxford University Press, 1947).

THE EDUCATIONAL THOUGHT AND INFLUENCE OF MATTHEW ARNOLD, by W. F. Connell (Routledge, 1950).

MATTHEW ARNOLD THE ETHNOLOGIST, by F. E. Faverty (North-western University Press, 1951). A study of Arnold's use of current racialist notions in ON THE STUDY OF CELTIC LITERA-TURE and elsewhere.

THE VICTORIAN SAGE: STUDIES IN ARGUMENT, by John Holloway (Macmillan, 1953). Contains an analysis of Arnold's methods of persuasion in his prose writings.

THE ALIEN VISION OF VICTORIAN POETRY, by E. D. H. Johnson (Princeton University Press, 1952). Contains a long essay on Arnold's poetry as an expression of the dilemma of the artist in modern society.

REVALUATION, by F. R. Leavis (Chatto and Windus, 1936). The note entitled 'Arnold, Wordsworth and the Georgians' is brief but important.

THE POETRY OF MATTHEW ARNOLD: A COMMENTARY, by C. B. Tinker and H. F. Lowry (Oxford University Press, 1940). An informative handbook for readers of Arnold's poems.

MATTHEW ARNOLD, by Lionel Trilling (Allen and Unwin, 1939). A critical study of Arnold's thought in relation to that of his age.

NINETEENTH CENTURY STUDIES, by Basil Willey (Chatto and Windus, 1949). Includes essays on Dr. Arnold and Matthew Arnold, each written with special reference to its subject's religious views.

INDEX